Maura Laverty

Novelist, journalist, playwright, storyteller supreme,
Maura Laverty always had an interest in cooking, a love
that peeps out of almost everything she ever wrote.

Born in Rathdangan in County Kildare in 1907, she
went to Spain at the age of seventeen as a governess but
soon graduated to secretarial work, and began to write
for a Madrid newspaper. A whirlwind romance with an
Irish journalist led to marriage and three children. She
continued writing and her first novel *Never No More*,
published in 1942, was an immediate success. She
published three more novels (all banned in Ireland until
the 1960s), two children's books and her well-known
cookbooks. One of her novels, dramatised as *Liffey Lane*,
was produced by Hilton Edwards and Michael
MacLiammoir. Another play, *Tolka Row*, became a very
popular television series on RTE. She died in 1966.

Full and Plenty, her most comprehensive cookbook,
was first published in 1960.

MAURA LAVERTY'S

Full & Plenty

ANVIL BOOKS

First published in 1960
Second edition 1966
This edition 1985
by Anvil Books
45 Palmerston Road, Dublin 6.
Reprinted 1991
Reprinted 1993.

ISBN 0 900068 99 X

Irish countryside (cover), courtesy of Bord Fáilte
Illustrations Terry Myler
Typesetting by Computertype Limited
Printed by Colour Books Limited

Contents

Useful facts and figures

Ounces don't translate into convenient metric measures. In this book they are rounded up or down to the nearest 25 grams; the table shows the exact equivalent to the nearest round figure, and the conversion used in the book.

Ounces – grams

Ounces	g equivalent	Conversion
½	14	13
1	28	25
2	57	50
3	85	75
4	113	100
5	142	150
6	170	175
7	198	200
8	227	225
9	255	250
10	283	275
11	312	300
12	340	350
13	368	375
14	397	400
15	425	425
16 (1 lb)	454	450
17	482	475
18	510	500
19	539	535
20 (1¼ lb)	567	560
24 (1½ lb)	681	675

The imperial tablespoon (Irish and English) holds approx. 17 ml. The American holds only 14 ml, and the Australian 20 ml. The teaspoon is the same in all countries.

Oven temperatures

Gas mark	F°	C°
½	250	120
1	275	140
2	300	150
3	325	165
4	350	175
5	375	190
6	400	200
7	425	220
8	450	230
9	475	240
10	500	250

The imperial (and Australian) pint is 20 fluid ounces; the American pint is 16 fluid ounces.

Liquids

Imperial	Approx. ml	Conversion
1 tbs	15	15
¼ pint	142	150
½ pint	283	275
¾ pint	426	425
1 pint	568	570
1½ pint	852	850
1¾ pint	1000	1000

Handy measures (all level tablespoons)

1 oz butter/sugar	2 tablespoons	⅛ cup
2 oz butter/sugar	4 tablespoons	¼ cup
4 oz butter/sugar	8 tablespoons	½ cup
8 oz butter/sugar	16 tablespoons	1 cup
1 oz flour	4 tablespoons	
2 oz flour	8 tablespoons	½ cup
4 oz flour	16 tablespoons	1 cup

Introduction

I love kitchens. The preparation of food has always been to me what literature or music or painting is to others. It is such a kindly, friendly, unselfish art, the art of cooking, and every little step in the preparation of even the plainest dish is an opportunity for self-expression. That sprinkling of chopped parsley beaten into the mashed potatoes is so much more than the final touch demanded by the cookery books. It is the satisfaction of your natural craving for all green-and-white things, things like the tips of grass spears piercing the snow on a morning in January. It is the expression of your wish to share these things with the people you are feeding. Glaze the top of an apple-tart and you are not merely adding sweetness and a deeper colour to the crust. You are voicing your love for all that is burnished and golden and gladdening in Nature and in people and in art.

Cooking is the poetry of housework. But it is satisfying in twenty other different ways as well. There is a grand warm companionable feeling to be got out of the thought that every time you baste a roast or beat an egg, or do any other little ordinary kitchen job, you are making yourself one with the Grand Order of Homemakers, past, present, and to come. And it does your nerves a world of good. Peel a basket of apples and watch the soothed feeling that comes over you as the knife slides smoothly between skin and juicy flesh — round after round, round after round, till each peel drops in a long unbroken curl. Or rub butter into flour for scones — there is something that I would recommend to neurotic people as a better tonic than anything their doctors could give them. The purity of flour, the cool velvety feel of it, the gentle, incessant calm-giving motion of the finger-tips — no tangle or turmoil could hold out against such homely comforting.

To sum up: Good cooking depends on four main factors — goodwill on the part of the cook, good kitchen equipment, good ingredients and good recipes. In this book, you will find the cream of the cooking lore I have acquired through the years. Every recipe has been tested by me and approved and enjoyed by my family and friends.

Bread

'I believe in bread-making' is the first and most important article of my culinary Credo. I applaud every effort to revive this kindliest of domestic arts. My enthusiasm is not based on health reasons alone. I believe in the traditional goodness of bread. I believe that the woman who bakes her family's bread brings this goodness into the kitchen. Did you know that gypsies often lay a crust of bread on the breast of a corpse? They do not intend the bread as food for the next world. It is just that they look on bread as a holy substance. 'The dear God's bread,' they call it. Their habit of carrying a crust in their pocket as a protection against evil spirits dates from Elizabethan times. There is a couplet by Herrick which goes:

> *In your pocket for a trust,*
> *Carry nothing but a crust,*
> *For that holy piece of bread*
> *Charms the danger and the dread.*

And plain bread *can* charm — as Mrs. Donnelly discovered to her chagrin that time Brian Feeney was courting the domestic economy instructress who is now his happy wife.

Brian's mother was more sincere than is usual with widowed mothers of only sons when she said she would be glad to see Brian bring in a wife. 'I'm poor company for him,' she often said. 'And in a big old place like this, there's more work than can be managed by an elderly woman like myself with only a raw servant girl to give her a hand.'

That was why she was genuinely pleased when Brian, at thirty-five, suddenly showed all the signs and symptoms of a man who is courting. Mrs. Feeney passed no remark when he took to shaving himself every evening when the cows were milked and the supper was over. She never once asked him where he was going when, changed from his working clothes into his Sunday suit, he set off on his bicycle down the New-bridge road. In her heart she may have said, 'Heaven grant she's a nice girl who'll make him happy,' or, 'May she bring peace and content into this house, whoever she is.' But, though she felt a natural curiosity, she had little anxiety. She knew that she could trust her son, and that he would tell her all she ought to know whenever the time would be ripe.

Mrs. Donnelly anticipated him with the news.

There were few in Ballyderrig who welcomed the coming of Mrs. Donnelly. 'The Raven' she was called. She well deserved her nickname. Never did a bird of ill-omen take more delight in carrying news that was calculated to disturb and alarm.

That Sunday afternoon when she called on Mrs. Feeney, she came with a pound of blackcurrant jam and a stone of sympathy. Carefully, she lowered her bulk on to a chair which, under her overflowing width, took on the aspect of doll's house furiture. She sighed gustily. The chair creaked loudly.

'Do you know what it is, Mary?' she opened. 'The longer I live, the more I realise that I'm as well off to be childless.'

'Why do you say that, Sarah?' Mrs. Feeney asked with kindness.

'For the simple reason that I'm able to enjoy my old age in comfort without being upset by the carryings-on of young people.' Mrs. Donnelly's broad face was wreathed in complacency. 'My heart goes out to every unfortunate woman with a marriageable son.'

'Ah, I don't know, now,' Mrs. Feeney said reasonably. 'Take my Brian. He never gave me an hour's worry in his life.'

This was the opening for which Mrs. Donnelly had been manoeuvring. She leaned forward, a podgy hand planted on either knee. 'Heaven help you, Mary,' she sympathised. 'It's little you know how he's planning to bring a strange woman in on top of you.'

'Oh, *that*?' There was relief in Mrs. Feeney's voice. For a second or two, Sarah Donnelly had had her worried. 'For Brian to take a wife would be no upset to me, Sarah. I'm more than pleased that he's showing signs of being interested in some girl in Newbridge.'

Mrs. Donnelly was annoyed. So this was the way Mary Feeney was going to take it? So she was going to make out that she didn't care? Mrs. Feeney smiled her gentle smile. 'I'll be happy to welcome Brian's wife. I know that he'll bring no woman in here except one that's suitable.'

Mrs. Donnelly shook her head in sad commiseration. 'Heaven give you sense, you creature,' she said. 'Brian is going to shame and humiliate you.'

Satisfaction gushed in her as she saw alarm leap at last into Mary Feeney's eyes, and when she heard the other woman's urgent, 'Who is she? Who or what is she, Sarah?'

'A domestic economy instructress — that's what she is!' Mrs. Donnelly sat back. 'She's a high-falutin' lassie with strings of letters after her name. A college-trained cook with classy notions about dressed-up dishes, who'll come in here and make little of your cooking, and who'll make your son wonder how he ever managed to reach manhood on the food you fed him. Heaven comfort you, Mary Feeney, because it's comfort you'll be needing.'

There was little that Mrs. Feeney could say. Put as Sarah Donnelly had put it, the situation offered poor prospect of her being able to go to her grave in peace and contentment. She realised now that her happy acceptance of Brian's courtship had been based on visions of herself imparting all she knew of home-making to a girl who would look up to her and respect her and treat her as an oracle. The thought of having to make way for a scornful college-trained cook filled her with woe.

She was plunged into deeper woe when Brian came to her a few days later to tell her the news he thought she would be delighted to hear. 'You'll love Anna, mother,' he said. 'She's a grand girl — a girl after your own heart. I'd like to bring her over to tea next Sunday.'

When Mrs. Donnelly called that evening, she found Mary

Feeney sitting, depressed and worried, with a cookery book in her hand. 'It's what to give her for her tea that has me distracted,' she confessed, patting her soft grey hair in an agitated way. 'If it was dinner, now. But I'm the worst hand in the world when it comes to making fancy cakes.'

It was true. As was the case with most of the farming women of Ballyderrig, the making of fancy cakes was as foreign to Mrs. Feeney as going upstairs to bed is foreign to a tinker. Plain bread was a different story. When it came to making plain soda bread, there was no one in the County Kildare who could hold a candle to her. The dough of her bread was as light and as white as bog cotton. The crust was always brittle and richly brown, with never a crack or a seam. The shape had a symmetry usually to be seen only in advertisements, and the flavour was the true sweet nutty flavour of perfectly baked wheat.

But while good soda bread was all right in its way, it would not suffice of itself to make an attractive tea-table, particularly when the guest of honour was a girl on whom Mrs. Feeney had to make a good impression. More particularly still when that girl was a domestic economy teacher who had learned all there is to be known about the grandeur of stylish confectionery.

'You're in a sad fix, to be sure,' Mrs. Donnelly sympathised. 'Isn't it the pity of the world that you never mastered the making of sweet cakes? A nice sponge cake like mine, or a nice marble cake like the one I make with four eggs — that's the kind of cake to make an elegant tea-table that wouldn't bring shame on a woman before her future daughter-in-law, even if she were to have all the letters of the alphabet after her name.'

'What will I do, at all?' Mrs. Feeney lamented.

'And isn't it a most unfortunate thing,' Mrs. Donnelly pursued relentlessly, 'to be living in a backward place like this where a nice fancy cake is not to be bought? You could, of course, send in to Newbridge or Kildare for one. But how would you be sure that it wouldn't be stale? Or that what went into it wasn't of the cheapest quality? A trained instructress would be the first to notice a thing like that.'

Mrs. Feeney threw herself on The Raven's mercy. She pleaded, 'Sarah, would you ever make a couple of cakes for me? A couple of real nice ones? I'll give you all the butter and eggs and sugar you want.'

'With pleasure,' Mrs. Donnelly said, and she meant it. She would enjoy telling Ballyderrig how Mary Feeney had had to call on her for help.

'You'll come to tea yourself on Sunday?' Mrs. Feeney invited, since there was no way out of it.

'With pleasure,' Sarah Donnelly repeated. To be able to give a first-hand account of the new Mrs. Feeney would be better still.

If appearance and manner were all that counted, Mrs. Feeney would have said that Anna Shiels was the daughter-in-law for whom she had been praying. She was a slim, brown-haired girl with good grey eyes and with the merry gentleness of a wren. It gave the elderly woman great happiness to see the way she looked at Brian and he at her.

The table looked nice. Mrs. Donnelly had made a sponge cake with a swirl of white icing to crown it, and her famous marble cake had risen nicely. For those who might like a bite of something plain to start, there was a plate of Mrs. Feeney's soda bread, thinly cut and well buttered.

Anna Shiels was one of those who like to start their tea with plain bread. She took a slice, and then another slice, and another slice after that.

'Here, have a bit of sweet cake,' Mrs. Donnelly urged. 'What about a scrap of sponge? Or, a nice slice of marble cake?'

'I'd rather have this delicious soda bread, thanks,' Anna said, helping herself to yet another slice. 'I never tasted the like of it in my life. It would win a prize anywhere. How on earth do you make it, Mrs. Feeney?'

Pride and happiness dawned like the rising sun in Mrs. Feeney's face. 'It's simple,' she explained eagerly. 'Just take the full of the little blue jug of milk, as much as you think of flour, a taste of salt and a suspicion of bread soda. And then you mix it — but you don't wet it, if you know what I mean.'

Anna said seriously, 'I always think it's in the cooking of plain food that a real cook proves herself. Take sweet cakes, now. Any child could make a sweet cake that will pass. It stands to reason that if you mix up a lot of nice tasting things like eggs and butter and sugar you'll be bound to have something that will taste nice, particularly if you put a slather of icing over it. But there's no way of disguising badly made soda bread. Yours is a real treat, Mrs. Feeney. Would you think me very greedy if I had another slice?'

'Eat away, alanna,' Mrs. Feeney said, her heart dancing to this sweet music.

'You know,' Anna confided, 'it's only after leaving college that a girl like myself finds out all she has to learn. Anyone at all can cook in a city kitchen where there's nothing to be done but look after the stove. But the cook who really deserves admiration is the woman who can turn out good food in a farmhouse kitchen in between churning and feeding calves and fowl. How does she ever manage to get around it all?'

'No difficulty at all, Anna,' Mrs. Feeney assured her, and her eyes were shining. 'No difficulty in the world, child. All a young married woman needs is to have someone experienced at hand to give her advice now and again and to show her the way.'

When the tea was over and Brian stood up to go out to the milking, Mrs. Donnelly decided that it was time for her to leave. 'Good evening to you all,' she said shortly, as she left.

Mrs. Feeney and Anna did not miss her company. They had a very enjoyable time looking through photographs of Brian as a baby.

Soda bread

Soda bread is the traditional bread of Ireland and our greatest gift to international cuisine. It appears on breakfast and tea-tables the length and breadth of Ireland, and is the perfect accompaniment to another great Irish speciality, smoked salmon.

Soda bread can be either white or brown, and in Ireland is usually made with buttermilk. If you can't get buttermilk, milk from the buttermilk plant (recipe follows) can be used. Sour milk is also a substitute.

White Irish soda bread is made from ordinary white flour. Brown soda bread is made with wholemeal flour, sometimes called wheaten flour or wheaten meal, and means ground wheat composed of 100% wheat kernel. Although it is possible to make excellent bread of wholemeal alone, most cooks like to add a small proportion of white flour so as to secure better cutting consistency.

It is important to get the dough to the right consistency. The mixture should not be too dry. On the other hand, too much liquid makes heavy bread. Only experience will teach you the exact amount.

Soda bread is always 'crossed' on the top, to keep it from cracking in the baking. The cuts should go over the sides of the cake to make sure of this.

I have given approximate times for cooking but the real test is to tap the bottom of the cake. If it sounds hollow, it is done.

Note: Some people like to add ¼ teaspoon of cream of tartar or ½ teaspoon of baking powder. I think this is unnecessary. The teaspoon of bread soda and good buttermilk provide all the leaven needed.

Buttermilk plant	1 oz sugar (25 g)
	1 oz yeast (25 g)
	1 quart tepid milk and water (1 litre)

Cream sugar and yeast and gradually add the tepid milk and water. Cover and leave for two days at room temperature or until the milk smells and tastes like buttermilk. When you want to use the milk for drinking or baking, strain it through a colander lined with butter muslin. A residue resembling thin lumpy cornflour will remain in the muslin. Gently pour over it a cup of tepid water so as to rinse off all sour milk. To start off a new lot of buttermilk, scrape the 'plant' from the muslin, place it in a scalded vessel and add 1 quart of tepid milk and water. Cover it, and leave it as before in a warm place to increase and multiply.

That first ounce of yeast will go on growing, giving you buttermilk until the end of time. But the 'plant' must be given a certain amount of care.

(1) It must be strained at least every five days.

(2) Make sure that the milk-and-water mixture is never more than tepid. Strong heat kills yeast.

(3) Cleanliness is very important. The careful rinsing after straining and the scalding of the container are necessary if the 'plant' is to live.

When using milk from the buttermilk plant, it doesn't hurt the bread to let it stand for about 15 minutes before baking.

Soda bread (basic recipe)

1 lb flour (450 g)
1 teaspoon salt
1 teaspoon sugar
1 teaspoon bread soda
Buttermilk to mix

Sift the dry ingredients together several times. Make a well in the centre and pour in the buttermilk gradually, mixing in the flour from the sides. Turn on to a floured board and knead lightly for a few minutes. Form into a round cake. Cross the top, brush with milk and put into a hot oven on a baking tin for about 45 minutes at 450° (gas mark 8).

Griddle bread

Using the basic mixture, roll out the dough 1 inch thick. Cut it into four farls or quadrant wedges. Cook them on a hot floured griddle or pan, 10 minutes on one side, 10 on the other.

Seedy bread

Increase the sugar to 1 tablespoon, and rub 2 oz (50 g) of

butter into the flour. Add 1 dessertspoon of caraway seeds.

Treacle bread
Increase the sugar to 1 tablespoon, and add to the buttermilk half a cup of treacle. A beaten egg may be added as well, and 2 oz (50 g) of butter rubbed into the flour. Raisins, currants and chopped nuts make this a party cake.

Wholemeal bread (1)

4 oz white flour (110 g)
1 teaspoon salt
1 teaspoon bread soda
1¼ lb wholemeal (560 g)
Buttermilk to mix

Sieve together the white flour, salt and soda. Mix well with the wholemeal. Make a well in the centre and gradually mix in sufficient liquid to make a stiff dough. Turn on to a floured board and knead lightly until free from cracks. Form into a round cake, and cross. Bake at once in a 450° oven (gas mark 8). for 60 minutes.

Wholemeal bread (2)

¾ teaspoon salt
1 dessertspoon castor sugar
1 teaspoon bread soda
4 oz white flour (110g)
12 oz wholemeal (350g)
Buttermilk to mix

Sift together the salt, sugar, bread soda and white flour. Mix thoroughly with the wheaten meal. Add sufficient buttermilk to make a stiff dough. Press the dough lightly into a greased loaf tin and bake for about 45 minutes in a 450° oven (gas mark 8).

To freshen bread: Roll in foil and place in a moderate oven for about 6 minutes

Fruit loaves

Use a well-greased loaf pan. Having baked the loaf for the time specified in the recipe, test for doneness (since ovens vary). To test: Insert a toothpick in the centre; if it comes out clean, the loaf is cooked.

Most fruit loaves have a crack on the top crust — this is characteristic and is not a fault. Do not cut a fruit loaf for 24 hours after baking.

Apricot nut loaf

1 lb. flour (450g)
¾ teaspoon salt
2 teaspoons baking powder
2 oz butter or margarine (50g)
2 oz sugar (50g)
1 teaspoon grated orange rind
6 oz finely chopped apricots (175g)
2 tablespoons chopped nuts
1 egg
¾ pint milk (425ml)
1 tablespoon orange juice

Sift together the flour, salt and baking powder. Rub in the butter. Add the sugar, orange rind, apricots and nuts. Mix the egg with the milk and orange juice. Add to the flour and mix well. Bake for 60–70 minutes in a moderate oven (350°, gas mark 4).

Boston brown bread (steamed)

8 oz flour (225g)
4 oz wheaten meal (110g)
4 oz Indian meal (110g)
1 teaspoon baking powder
1 teaspoon bread soda
1 teaspoon salt
¾ pint buttermilk (425 ml)
4 tablespoons treacle
6 oz sultanas (175g)

Mix together in a bowl, the flour, wheaten meal and Indian meal. Add the baking powder, bread soda and salt. Make a well in the centre. Combine the buttermilk with the treacle and the sultanas. Add all at once to the dry ingredients and stir just sufficiently to moisten all the flour.

Thoroughly grease 3 cylindrical tins (such as baby food containers), and pour an equal amount of batter into each of the tins. Cut squares of greaseproof paper large enough to cover the tops of the tins and come down about 1½ inches on the sides. Grease the paper and tie it on securely.

Put a rack in the bottom of a large saucepan and stand the tins on the rack. Pour sufficient boiling water into the pot to come no more than half-way up the sides of the tins. Put the lid on the pot and bring the water to the boil. Reduce heat to a simmer, and steam the bread for 3 hours. (After about an hour, it may be necessary to add additional boiling water to keep the water at the half-way level.)

When the bread is cooked, run a spatula carefully down and around the inside of the tins to loosen the bread. Turn out on to a rack and leave to cool. When cool, wrap in greaseproof paper and keep for 24 hours before using.

Bran date loaf

8 oz dates (225g)
2 cups boiling water
2 eggs
6 tablespoons brown sugar
12 oz wheaten meal (350g)
1 teaspoon baking powder
1 teaspoon bread soda
6 ozs bran (175g)
1 teaspoon vanilla

Stone and chop the dates, and pour the boiling water over them. In a separate bowl beat the eggs until light. Add the brown sugar slowly, stirring constantly. When the eggs and sugar are creamy, sift in half of the wheaten meal, with the baking powder and bread soda. Add half of the date mixture. When well mixed, add the remainder of the wheaten meal, the bran and vanilla. Add the remaining date mixture and mix lightly. Place the dough in a lightly greased tin. Bake for 1 hour in a moderate oven at 350° (gas mark 4).

Bran treacle loaf

6 oz bran (175g)
8 oz wheaten meal (225g)
1 teaspoon baking powder
1 teaspoon salt
1 teaspoon bread soda
1 egg
4 tablespoons treacle
¾ pint buttermilk (425 ml)
6 oz raisins (175 g)

Combine the bran, wheaten meal, baking powder, salt and bread soda. Combine and beat the egg, treacle and buttermilk. Add the liquid to the dry ingredients and add the raisins. Divide the batter between 2 greased oblong loaf tins and bake for 40 minutes in a 375° oven (gas mark 5).

Date and nut loaf

½ pint boiling water (275 ml)
4 oz dates (110g)
4 oz brown sugar (110g)
1 oz. butter or margarine (25g)
1 egg
8 oz flour (225g)
½ teaspoon bread soda
¾ teaspoon baking powder
½ teaspoon salt
2 oz chopped nuts (50g)

Pour the boiling water over the chopped and stoned dates and leave to cool. Mix the sugar, butter and egg throughly. Stir in the dates and the water. Sift and stir in the flour, soda, baking powder and salt. Blend in the chopped nuts. Pour the mixture into a well-greased loaf pan and let it stand for 15 minutes before baking. Bake for 40–50 minutes in a moderate oven at 350° (gas mark 4).

Fruit loaf

4 oz flour (110g)
12 oz wheaten meal (350g)
2 teaspoons baking powder
¼ teaspoon salt
2 oz brown sugar (50g)

8 oz raisins (225g)
2 eggs
1 cup of milk

Sift the dry ingredients, and add the raisins. Combine the beaten eggs and the milk, and add to the dry mixture. Mix only enough to moisten the flour. Turn into a greased tin and bake at 350° (gas mark 4) for 50–60 minutes.

Gingerbread loaf

6 oz flour (175g)
½ teaspoon bread soda
½ teaspoon ground ginger
3 oz rice flour (75g)
2 oz butter (50g)
2 oz ground almonds (50g)
4 oz raisins (110g)
2 oz candied peel (50g)
2 oz treacle (50g)
3 tablespoons sour milk (45 ml)
1 egg

Sift the flour, bread soda and ginger, and mix with the rice flour. Rub in the butter. Add the ground almonds, halved raisins and sliced peel. Mix the treacle with the milk and well-beaten egg, and stir into the dry ingredients. Turn into a well-buttered tin and bake for 1¼ hours at 375°, (gas mark 5).

Nut and raisin loaf

1 egg
4 oz sugar (110g)
4 tablespoons milk (60 ml)
8 oz flour (225g)
1 teaspoon baking powder
⅛ teaspoon salt
4 oz chopped raisins (110g)
4 oz chopped nuts (110g)

Mix the beaten egg with the sugar and the milk. Gradually stir in the flour, which has been sifted with the baking powder and the salt. Add the fruit and nuts and mix well. Turn into a greased tin and bake for 50 minutes at 400° (gas mark 6).

Orange nut loaf

6 oz sugar (175g)
2 oz butter or margarine (50g)
1 egg
$\frac{1}{2}$ pint milk (275 ml)
$\frac{1}{4}$ pint orange juice (150ml)
4 teaspoons grated orange rind
12 oz flour (350g)
$\frac{3}{5}$ teaspoon salt
$1\frac{1}{2}$ teaspoons baking powder
4 oz chopped nuts (100g)

Cream the sugar and the butter, then add the beaten egg. Stir in the milk, orange juice and orange rind, and then the flour which has been sieved with the salt and the baking powder. Blend in the nuts. Turn into a greased tin, and bake for 70 minutes at 350° (gas mark 4).

Prune loaf

4 oz dried prunes (110g)
6 oz sugar (175g)
2 oz butter or margarine (50g)
1 egg
4 tablespoons milk (60 ml)
$\frac{1}{2}$ pint of liquid from prunes (275ml)
12 oz flour (350g)
$1\frac{1}{2}$ teaspoons baking powder
$\frac{3}{4}$ teaspoon salt

Cook the prunes in just enough water to cover them; when soft, drain and reserve the water. Stone and chop the drained prunes. Mix thoroughly the sugar, butter and beaten egg. Stir in the milk and the prune juice. Add the sifted flour, baking powder and salt. Blend in the chopped prunes. Turn into a greased tin, and bake for about 70 minutes at 350°, (gas mark 4).

Prune and raisin bread

1 lb flour (450g)
$\frac{1}{2}$ teaspoon mixed spice.
$\frac{1}{2}$ teaspoon nutmeg
$\frac{1}{2}$ teaspoon salt
$1\frac{1}{2}$ teaspoons baking powder

2 oz sugar (50g)
4 oz butter or margarine (110g)
8 oz raisins (225g)
4 oz chopped prunes (110g)
2 eggs
½ pint milk (275 ml)

Sift the flour, spices, salt, baking powder and sugar. Rub in the butter finely. Add the fruit, and then the beaten eggs and milk. Mix well. Turn into a greased tin and bake for 1½ hours in a moderate oven (375°, gas mark 5).

Seed loaf

1 lb flour (450g)
1½ teaspoons baking powder
¼ teaspoon salt
4 oz butter or margarine (110g)
4 oz sugar (110g)
1 dessertspoon caraway seeds
1 egg
Milk to mix

Sift the flour, baking powder and salt. Rub in the butter. Add the sugar and the caraway seeds, and mix thoroughly. Add the beaten egg and enough milk to make a light dough that will drop from the spoon. Turn into a greased tin and bake for about 1¼ hours in a moderate oven (375°, gas mark 5).

Seed luncheon loaf

1 lb flour (450g)
2 teaspoons baking powder
¼ teaspoon salt
4 oz margarine (110g)
2 oz butter (50g)
6 oz sugar (175g)
1 teaspoon caraway seeds
3 oz candied peel (75g)
2 eggs
Milk to mix

Sift together the flour, baking powder and salt. Rub in the margarine and the butter. Add the sugar, seeds and thinly sliced peel, and then the beaten eggs, with just enough milk to make a light dough. Place in a well-greased tin and bake for 1½ hours in a moderate oven (375°, gas mark 5).

Sultana loaf	8 oz flour (225g)
	¼ teaspoon salt
	1 teaspoon baking powder
	3 oz butter or margarine (75g)
	4 oz castor sugar (110g)
	2 oz chopped walnuts (50g)
	4 oz sultanas (110g)
	⅓ pint milk (190 ml)
	1 whole egg
	1 egg yolk

Sift the flour, salt and baking powder, then rub in the butter. Add the sugar, nuts and sultanas and mix well. Combine the milk and the eggs, which have been well beaten. Stir into the mixture and mix well. Pour into a well-buttered loaf tin and bake for 60 minutes in a moderate oven (375°, gas mark 5). Leave for 24 hours before cutting, then cut in thin slices and butter well.

Sultana loaf (spiced)	1 lb flour (450g)
	4 oz sugar (110g)
	¼ teaspoon salt
	1½ teaspoons baking powder
	¼ teaspoon cinnamon
	¼ teaspoon ginger
	8 oz butter or margarine (225g)
	8 oz sultanas (225g)
	2 oz candied peel (50g)
	2 eggs
	Milk to mix
	A few blanched almonds

Sift together the flour, sugar, salt, baking powder and spices. Rub in the butter until the mixture looks like fine bread-crumbs. Add the sultanas and thinly sliced peel and mix thoroughly. Add the eggs which have been well-beaten, and just enough milk to make a dough that will drop from the spoon. Turn into a well-greased tin, arrange a few halved blanched almonds on top and bake for 1½ hours in a moderate oven (375°, gas mark 5).

Treacle bread	3 tablespoons treacle
	¼ pint milk (150ml)
	2 oz butter or margarine (50g)
	2 oz brown sugar (50g)
	8 oz flour (225g)
	¾ teaspoon baking powder
	1 tablespoon ground ginger
	1 egg
	1 oz castor sugar (25g)

Mix the treacle and the milk, and warm slightly. Cream the butter and sugar, and add to the treacle mixture. Sift together the flour, baking powder and ground ginger, and add gradually to the creamed mixture, beating well. Then add the beaten egg. Pour into a greased flat tin lined with greased paper. Bake for 1 hour in a moderate oven (375°, gas mark 5). When cold, cut in squares and sift castor sugar on top.

Treacle fruit loaf	2 oz butter or margarine (50g)
	2 tablespoons treacle
	¼ pint sour milk (150 ml)
	1 teaspoon bread soda
	½ teaspoon salt
	3 oz sugar (75g)
	1 egg
	1 lb wholemeal flour (450g)
	6 oz sultanas (175g)

Melt the butter, add the treacle and the milk and stir well. Sift the flour with the bread soda and the salt, and add the sugar. Add the beaten egg to the milk mixture. Then gradually add the flour, mixing well. Stir in the fruit. Turn into a well-greased tin and bake for 1¼ hours in a moderate oven (375°, gas mark 5).

Muffins

For the perfect muffin, even of texture, symmetrical of shape, moist of crumb and light as bog-cotton, two things are necessary: Discretion in beating, and moderation in baking. Do not beat more than is necessary to blend the ingredients. If there are lumps in the mixture ignore them; they will disappear in the cooking. The secret of tender muffins is speed in the mixing. And never let the oven temperature go above 425° (gas mark 7). When cooked, remove immediately from tins, using a sharp knife or spatula. Serve hot.

To reheat muffins, wrap in aluminium foil and place in a moderately hot oven for 5 minutes.

Basic muffin recipe

8 oz flour (225g)
½ teaspoon salt
2 tablespoons castor sugar
1 teaspoon baking powder
2 eggs
2 oz soft butter or margarine (50g)
6 tablespoons milk (90ml)

Sift the flour with the salt, sugar and baking powder. Combine the beaten eggs with the butter and milk. Stir quickly into the flour mixture. Pour the batter at once into well-greased muffin tins (they should be about two-thirds full). Bake for 15–20 minutes at 425° (gas mark 7).

Variations
These use the same basic muffin recipe and are baked in the same way.

Apple muffins
Fold 4 oz (110g) finely chopped raw apples into the basic mixture. On top of each muffin, place a slice of raw apple coated with a mixture of 4 parts castor sugar to 1 part ground cinnamon.

Banana muffins
Add 3 tablespoons diced banana to basic recipe.

Date muffins
Add 3 tablespoons chopped dates and 1 tablespoon chopped nuts to basic recipe.

Apricot muffins

2 oz soft butter or margarine (50g)
2 oz brown sugar (50g)
1 egg
6 tablespoons milk (90 ml)
8 oz flour (225g)
½ teaspoon salt
1 teaspoon baking powder
3 oz finely chopped, cooked and
   drained apricots (75g)

Cream the butter and sugar and beat in the egg. Add the milk alternately with the sifted dry ingredients. Fold in the apricots. Pour the batter into well-greased and lightly-floured tins. Bake for 25 minutes at 400° (gas mark 6).

Crumb muffins

1 teacup dry breadcrumbs
6 tablespoons milk (90ml)
4 oz sultanas (110g)
3 oz flour (75g)
¼ teaspoon salt
1 teaspoon baking powder
1 oz soft butter or margarine (25g)
1 egg

Soak the crumbs for 10 minutes in the milk. Add the sultanas, then the sifted dry ingredients. Quickly beat in the egg and butter. Bake for 20 minutes at 425° (gas mark 7).

Fraughan (blueberry) muffins

8 oz sifted flour (22gg)
1 teaspoon baking powder
4 oz castor sugar (110g)
¼ teaspoon salt
2 oz soft butter or margarine (50g)
1 breakfast cup fraughans
1 egg
¼ pint milk (150g)

Sift together the dry ingredients. Cut in the butter until barely blended. Add the fruit. Add the unbeaten egg and milk, and stir only until the ingredients are blended and the flour moistened. Fill greased muffin tins two-thirds full. Bake for 25 minutes in a moderately hot oven (400°, gas mark 6).

These muffins may be varied by omitting the fraughans and adding three-quarters of a cup of drained and chopped cherries or pineapple (fresh or tinned) to the basic mixture, or by adding half a cup of raisins, currants, figs, prunes or nuts.

Wholemeal muffins	2 ozs flour (50g)
	8 oz wheaten meal (225g)
	1 teaspoon baking powder
	3 ozs brown sugar (75g)
	½ teaspoon salt
	2 oz soft butter or margarine (50g)
	1 egg
	3 tablespoons milk (45 ml)

Sift the dry ingredients, then cut in the butter until barely blended. Add the egg and milk, and stir just enough to blend the ingredients. Fill well-greased muffin tins two-thirds full and bake for 20–25 minutes at 400° (gas mark 6).

Scones

If you can make good scones, then your tea-table will get along without fancy cakes. There are scores of ways in which plain scones may be dressed up to satisfy those with a sweet tooth. But they must be light, flaky and perfectly baked. Here are a few hints to ensure perfection.

(1) First of all, turn on the oven so that it will be pre-heated to 450° (gas mark 8).

(2) Assemble all the ingredients.

(3) Assemble all the utensils.

(4) Cut in whatever shortening you use with a pastry blender or two knives. Keep cutting until the mixture looks like coarse meal.

(5) Stir in almost all the milk. If the dough does not seem pliable, add the rest. Use sufficient milk to make a soft puffy

dough, easy to roll out.

(6) Round up the dough on a lightly floured cloth-covered board. (The cloth prevents the use of excess flour in rolling).

(7) Knead, that is, fold over the dough and press lightly with the heel of the hand, about 6 times. Handle lightly — too much handling will make scones tough. And even if the dough seems sticky, avoid adding flour in handling and rolling.

(8) Roll or pat out the dough. For a thin crusty scone, roll it about ⅓ inch thick. For a soft high scone, the dough should be ⅔ inch.

(9) Cut the dough with a floured cutter, or cut it in squares with a knife. Use a flat ungreased baking sheet. For soft-sided scones, place them close together. For crusty-sided scones, place them about 1 inch apart.

(10) Place the baking tin in the middle of the oven. A heavy or shiny pan will prevent over-browning on the bottom. For more even browning, line old tins with aluminium foil.

(11) Bake until golden brown (10–12 minutes).

(12) When scones are cooked, served immediately.

Basic scone recipe	12 oz flour (350g) ¾ teaspoon salt 1 teaspoon baking powder 1½ oz butter or margarine (40g) ⅔ cup milk (150ml)

Sift together the flour, salt and baking powder. Cut in the butter. Add the milk to make a soft dough. Knead, roll and cut out, then bake in a hot oven (450°, gas mark 8) for 10–12 minutes.

Apple scones

Add to the basic recipe 2 oz (50g) sugar and 1 cup of minced apples. Bind the mixture with a beaten egg. Mix well, put into a flat greased tin and bake for 25 minutes in a hot oven. When cooked, cut into sections; split, butter and serve hot. Dust the tops thickly with castor sugar.

Cinnamon rolls

Prepare the dough as in basic recipe. Roll to a rectangle ¼ inch thick. Spread to within ½ inch of the edge with a mixture of 2 tablespoons of brown sugar and 1 teaspoon of cinnamon — raisins may be added if you like. Roll up tightly as for a Swiss roll, beginning at the wide edge. Seal well by pinching the edges of the dough into the roll. Cut into 1 inch slices, and place these cut side down on a greased baking sheet or in greased muffin tins. Bake in a hot oven for about 20 minutes.

If you like, spread the warm baked scones with quick white icing made as follows: Sift a little icing sugar into a bowl, moisten with cream or milk to spreading consistency, and add ½ teaspoon of vanilla or other flavouring.

Devonshire scones
Make scones as in the basic recipe. Serve hot with butter, strawberry jam and whipped cream.

Fruit scones
To the basic recipe, add 4 oz (110g) of prepared raisins, sultanas or currants, or a mixture of all three. Bake for 12–15 minutes at 450° (gas mark 8).

Jam scones
Make dough according to the basic recipe and roll out ¼ inch thick. Cut into 3 inch rounds with floured cutter. Place a teaspoon of any jam in the centre, fold over, press the edges together tightly, and brush the tops with milk or beaten egg. Bake for 10–12 minutes in a hot oven (450°, gas mark 8).

Orange squares
Add 1 tablespoon of castor sugar and 1 teaspoon of orange rind to the dry ingredients of the basic recipe. Roll out and cut in 2 inch squares. Brush the tops of the squares with orange juice and sprinkle with ordinary sugar. Bake for 12 minutes at 475° (gas mark 9).

Orange tea scones
Add the grated rind of an orange to the dry ingredients of the basic recipe. Before baking, press into the top of each scone, ½ cube of loaf sugar which has been dipped in orange juice.

Buttermilk scones

Basic recipe

1 lb flour (450g)
1 teaspoon bread soda
½ teaspoon salt
3 oz butter or margarine (75g)
1 egg
¾ cup buttermilk or sour milk

Sift together the flour, bread soda and salt. Add the butter. Beat the egg slightly, add the milk, and mix with the dry ingredients. Roll out about ½ inch thick and cut with a floured cutter. Place on a greased tin. Bake for about 15 minutes at 475° (gas mark 9).

Cinnamon scones

1 recipe buttermilk scones
4 oz butter or margarine (110g)
4 oz brown sugar (110g)
2 teaspoons cinnamon
4 oz raisins (110g)

Make dough as in basic recipe, and roll it out ¼ inch thick. Brush with the softened butter, using about 1 oz. Sprinkle with 1 tablespoon of brown sugar, the cinnamon and raisins. Roll up like a Swiss roll, and cut in 2 inch pieces. Cream the remainder of the sugar and butter and spread the creamed mixture on the bottom and sides of a heavy baking tin. Place slices of dough in the tin, cut sides up. Allow to stand for 15 minutes, and then bake in a moderate oven (350°, gas mark 4) for 40 minutes. Invert the tin over a large dish, and leave for about 2 minutes to allow the caramel to drain on to the scones.

Fig rolls

1 recipe buttermilk scones
6 oz wholemeal flour (175g)
5 tablespoons brown sugar
2 oz soft butter (50g)
6 oz dried figs (175g)
Juice of ½ lemon

Make dough as for buttermilk scones, but substitute 6 oz of

wholemeal flour for 6 oz of white flour, and add 1 tablespoon brown sugar to the dry ingredients. Roll out ¼ inch thick, and spread with the remaining sugar, the butter, the figs, which have been finely chopped, and the lemon juice. Roll up like a Swiss roll, and cut into 12 slices. Place close together, cut side up, in a greased square baking tin. Bake for about 45 minutes in a moderate oven (350°, gas mark 4).

Marmalade scones

1 recipe buttermilk scones, reducing milk to 4 tablespoons (60 ml)
3 tablespoons marmalade

Make dough as in basic recipe but add the marmalade to the milk and beaten egg. Roll out the dough and cut in rounds. Top each with a little marmalade and bake for 15 minutes in a 425° oven (gas mark 7).

Pineapple fingers

1 recipe buttermilk scones
½ cup candied pineapple

Make dough as in basic recipe but add the candied pineapple, which has been finely chopped, to the dry ingredients. Roll out ¼ inch thick and sprinkle with granulated sugar. Cut into small finger-shaped pieces and place on a greased pan. Bake in a hot oven (475°, gas mark 9) for ten minutes.

Chopped candied peel, chopped dates or sultanas can be used instead of the pineapple.

Strawberry curls

1 recipe buttermilk scones
3 tablespoon castor sugar
2 tablespoons soft butter
8 oz strawberries (225g)

Make dough as for buttermilk scones, adding 1 tablespoon of castor sugar to the dry ingredients, and roll out ¼ inch thick. Spread with 2 tablespoons of soft butter. Slice the strawberries and sprinkle with 2 tablespoons of castor sugar. Cover the buttered dough with the strawberries. Roll up as for a Swiss roll. Cut in 1 inch slices and place in greased muffin pans, cut edges up. Bake for 25 minutes at 400° (gas mark 6)

Salad oil scones

These are extra rich and tender, with a delicate crispy crust top and bottom

12 oz flour (350g)
1 teaspoon baking powder
½ teaspoon salt
3 tablespoons salad oil (45 ml)
5 tablespoons milk (75 ml)

Sift together the dry ingredients. Pour the salad oil and the milk into a cup, but don't mix. Make a well in the centre of the dry ingredients and pour in the liquid all at once. Stir with a fork until the dough leaves the sides of the bowl clean. The dough will be rather sticky but do not add extra flour when kneading. Turn the dough on to a sheet of waxed paper. Lift the paper by one corner and fold dough over in half; press down firmly and pull paper back. Repeat with the other corners of the paper until the dough looks smooth. Roll out to ½ inch thick between 2 sheets of waxed paper. Cut with unfloured cutter and place on ungreased baking tin. Bake in a very hot oven (475°, gas mark 9) for 10–12 minutes.

You may, if you wish, use buttermilk instead of sweet milk for these scones. In this case, use ½ teaspoon of baking powder and ½ teaspoon bread soda.

Raisin topping

Delicious for all scones.

6 oz raisins (175g)
½ pint water (275 ml)
½ teaspoon grated lemon rind
4 oz sugar (110g)
1 tablespoon cornflour
1 dessertspoon lemon juice
1 tablespoon butter

Boil the raisins for 3 minutes in the water to which the lemon rind has been added. Mix the sugar with the cornflour and moisten with a little of the raisin mixture. Add to the raisins and cook for a further period, stirring constantly until the mixture boils and is clear. Add the lemon juice and butter and stir well. Use either hot or cold.

Griddle cakes (drop scones)

Some people call them drop scones; some call them griddle cakes. Whatever you call them, the first essential for these delicious made-in-a-minute teatime delicacies is a heavy iron frying-pan or griddle.

Some tips for perfect drop scones:

(1) It is important not to over-grease the pan — just rub with a cut turnip or a scrap of bacon fat. Test for correct heat by sprinkling the pan or griddle with a few drops of cold water. If the water splutters and 'dances' then the pan is ready.

(2) To ensure round, uniform cakes, pour the batter from the tip of a large spoon; for larger cakes, use a small jug with a lip, allowing plenty of room for spreading.

(3) When bubbles appear on the surface and burst, the cakes are ready for turning. Turn with a fish slice or spatula.

(4) Cook over moderate heat, allowing $2\frac{1}{2}$–3 minutes for each side.

(5) When both sides are browned, keep hot either in the oven between the folds of a clean tea-towel or between plates over a saucepan of simmering water.

(6) Keeping the batter in a refrigerator for 24 hours before cooking ensures light cakes.

Basic griddle cake recipe	12 oz flour (350g) 1 teaspoon baking powder $\frac{1}{2}$ teaspoon salt 1 oz castor sugar (25g) 2 eggs $\frac{3}{4}$ pint milk (425 ml) 2 oz butter or margarine (50g)

Sift together the flour, baking powder, salt and castor sugar. Combine the well-beaten eggs with the milk. Add to the flour mixture and beat until smooth. Add the melted butter. Bake as directed above and serve either with golden syrup or spread with butter and sprinkled with brown sugar.

Variations

All these use the basic recipe and are cooked in the same way.

Apple griddle cakes

To the basic recipe, add 1 cup of grated cooking apples and increase the sugar to 3 tablespoons. When cooked, spread with butter and sprinkle with castor sugar and cinnamon.

Banana griddle cakes

Slice one large ripe banana thinly and add to basic recipe. When cooked, spread with butter and sprinkle with sugar and lemon juice.

Dessert griddle cakes

Butter hot griddle cakes and serve with a sauce made by beating together until smooth equal parts of cream and raspberry or apricot jam.

Onion griddle cakes

Chop 1 large onion finely and fry gently until soft but do not let it brown. Add to basic griddle cake recipe (omitting the sugar), and cook. Serve with bacon and eggs.

Pineapple griddle cakes

Add 1 cup of drained crushed pineapple to basic recipe. When cooked, spread cakes with butter and dust with castor sugar.

Potato griddle cakes

Add 1 cup of grated raw potato to the basic recipe, omitting the sugar. When cooked, spread with butter creamed with 1 tablespoon of tomato ketchup.

Sultana griddle cakes

Steam 4 oz (110g) of prepared sultanas over hot water for about 5 minutes or until plump. When cold, add to the basic recipe. Serve hot with butter and sprinkled with castor sugar.

Breadcrumb griddle cakes

2 tablespoons butter or margarine
¾ pint scalded milk (425 ml)
1 breakfastcup fine breadcrumbs
2 eggs

4 oz flour (110g)
1 teaspoon baking powder
2 oz castor sugar (50g)
½ teaspoon salt
¾ teaspoon cinnamon

Add the softened butter to the scalded milk. Mix and pour over the breadcrumbs. Beat until smooth. Add the well-beaten eggs. Sift together the flour, baking powder, castor sugar, salt and cinnamon. Add to the butter, beat well and bake as directed. Spread with butter and sprinkle with brown sugar.

Christmas griddle cakes

4 oz butter or margarine (110g)
4 oz sugar (110g)
3 eggs
8 oz flour (225g)
1 teaspoon baking powder
⅛ teaspoon salt
Rind and juice of ½ lemon
4 oz currants (110g)

Work the butter and the sugar to a smooth cream, then slowly beat in the whole eggs, one at a time. Sift the flour with the baking powder and salt, and add a little, with the lemon rind and the juice, to the creamed mixture. Slowly beat in the rest of the flour and the currants (which have been mixed with some of the flour). Cook as in the basic recipe.

Oatmeal griddle cakes

4 oz flour (110g)
1 teaspoon baking powder
½ teaspoon salt
1 egg
1½ cups porridge
4 tablespoons milk
2 tablespoons water
2 tablespoons soft butter

Sift the flour, baking powder and salt. Add the well-beaten eggs, porridge, milk, water and soft butter. Beat until the batter is smooth. Cook as in the basic recipe.

Wholemeal griddle cakes	**12 oz wheaten meal (350g)** **1 teaspoon baking powder** **½ teaspoon salt** **4 oz butter or margarine (110g)** **Milk to mix**

Sift together the wheaten meal, baking powder and salt. Mix in the soft butter with a fork. Add sufficient milk to make a soft dough and mix well. Cook as in basic recipe.

Yeast bread

Editor's note: Maura Laverty used fresh yeast in her original recipes. She recognised, however, the advantages of dried yeast which keeps better and is more generally available than fresh yeast. The recipes that follow have been translated from fresh to dried yeast, using her measurement – 1 level tablespoon of dried yeast equals 1 oz of fresh yeast.

If you use fresh yeast, it is not necessary to reactivate it.

Soda bread may be the traditional bread of Ireland, but yeast bread has an important plus factor. When we add bicarbonate of soda to foods, we reduce their content of Vitamin B — the all-important vitamin necessary for muscular energy, steady nerves, healthy skin, good appetite, sound digestion. Because it is especially important to expectant and nursing mothers, it is known as 'the woman's vitamin'. Yeast is particularly rich in Vitamin B. It is also present in flour and in milk — which is why when we make bread with yeast we make three good things trebly valuable.

Yeast

Yeast comes in three forms — fresh, dried or powdered. As fresh yeast is often difficult to get and remains fresh for a relatively short time (about three days in a fridge) these recipes are for dried yeast which is readily available and keeps for about two months.

Yeast is a living organism but it is inactive until given warmth and water and, in the case of dried yeast, sugar.

So all recipes start with the activation of the dried yeast.

This is simple. Dissolve the sugar in hand-hot water, then whisk in the yeast and leave for about 10–15 minutes. A good froth or honeycomb of about an inch must form.

Two other factors affect the performance of yeast: Salt slows down the rising of the yeast so if you use more than given in the recipe, allow more time for rising. Fat also inhibits its growth so in recipes which require a richer dough (hot cross buns, for instance) extra yeast must be used.

Liquid

The mixing liquid for yeast breads can be water alone, milk alone, or a mixture of both, according to your taste. Milk gives a richer mixture, and the bread or buns have softer crusts.

Warmth

Warmth is important at all stages. The flour should be warm, the liquid hand-hot, utensils also warm. Most importantly, the dough needs a warm place if the yeast is to act. The top of a range or cooker, the airing cupboard or the plate warmer compartment may be suitable, but remember that if the temperature is too hot the yeast will be killed off and won't act. If you don't have a suitable warm spot, put the dough into a polythene bag, seal it and put it in a bowl of hot water. In suitable conditions the dough will rise in about 30 minutes; on the kitchen table it will take about three hours.

Kneading

The fineness of the texture of yeast bread depends on proper and thorough kneading. And there is more to this kneading than meets the eye! Push the dough from you with the heel of your fist and pull it towards you with your fingers. Keep turning it around clockwise as you knead. It is a one-two-three movement, and to do it properly you must get rhythm into it.

The dough should be elastic and even-textured.

Methods

There are two ways of making yeast bread. By using tepid liquid and leaving it in a warm place, you get a fairly rapid rise in bulk. If you use cold liquid, you can leave it overnight. The bread rises while you sleep, thus halving the work and the time involved.

White	**2–4 oz butter or margarine (50–110g)**
yeast bread	**1¾ pints tepid milk and water (1 litre)**
	1½ tablespoons dried yeast
	1 dessertspoon sugar
	3½ lb flour (1k575g)
	3½ teaspoons salt

Melt the butter in the milk and water mixture. Dissolve the sugar in about ½ pint of the liquid. Whisk in the yeast and leave to froth.

Warm the flour and sift with the salt. Make a well in the centre and pour in the frothing yeast. Mix to a smooth dough with the remainder of the milk and water, leaving the sides of the bowl clean, turn on to a floured board and knead well for at least 15 minutes.

When the bread is kneaded, put it back into the bowl, brush with butter, cover and leave in a warm place until it has doubled in bulk. Now knead it again, divide into two loaves, put them in greased loaf tins and brush with butter. Cover and again leave in a warm place until they have doubled their bulk. Into a hot oven with them now (500°, gas mark 10) to bake for one hour. Reduce the heat to 450° (gas mark 8) for the last 15 minutes of baking. Tap the bottom to make sure they are cooked. Stand them on their sides while cooling, and wrap them in tea-towels if you want a soft crust.

Yeast bread (overnight method)

The overnight, or cold-rising method of yeast bread-making, halves the work.

Prepare dough as for basic recipe but use cold milk or cold milk-and-water. Leave overnight to rise in a greased covered container. It is important to brush the top of the dough with butter as this prevents the formation of a skin which would check the rising of the dough. Next morning, turn the dough out on to a floured board and knead it lightly for a couple of minutes. Shape into loaves, place in greased tins and allow to rise for about 15 minutes. Bake as for basic recipe.

Wholemeal yeast bread

1½ tablespoons dried yeast
1 dessertspoon castor sugar
2 pints tepid milk and water
    (1150 ml)
3½ lb wholemeal flour (1kg 575g)
1 oz salt (25g)

Dissolve the sugar in about ½ pint of tepid liquid. Whisk in the yeast and leave to froth. Meanwhile warm the wholemeal and mix with the salt in a large warm basin. Make a well in the centre of the wholemeal and pour in the frothing yeast. Then stir with a wooden spoon until the meal is evenly moist (the dough should be wetter than when making wholemeal bread with soda).

Grease 3 large loaf tins and warm them well. Spoon in the dough (which should not be kneaded), cover with a cloth and leave in a warm place until half risen. Then bake for 50–60 minutes in a 450° oven (gas mark 8). When baked, turn the loaves upside down on a wire rack and leave until cold. If they do not come out easily, leave for a few minutes. Wholemeal bread is best kept for 24 hours before cutting.

Yeast rolls

8 oz flour (225g)
1 teaspoon salt
½ tablespoon dried yeast
1 teaspoon sugar
1 oz butter or margarine (25g)
¼ pint milk (150 ml)

Mix as for yeast bread, melting the butter in the warm milk. After kneading, shape into rolls. Place on a greased baking sheet and leave to prove (or rise a second time) for 20 minutes Brush with milk and bake for 20 minutes at 450° (gas mark 8).

Fancy yeast breads

Barmbrack

2 tablespoons dried yeast
1 teaspoon castor sugar
1½ pints warm milk-and-water
    (850 ml)

3 lbs flour (1kg 350g)
1 dessertspoon salt
1 teaspoon spice
4 oz butter or margarine (110g)
4 oz sugar (110g)
1 lb sultanas (450g)
4 oz currants (110g)
4 oz chopped peel (110g)

Dissolve the castor sugar in about a third of the milk and water. Whisk in the yeast and leave to froth. Prepare the fruit. Sieve the warmed flour, salt and spice into a large bowl and make a well in the centre. When ready, pour in the yeast mixture and the milk, and mix thoroughly. Knead to a ball, then turn out on to a floured board. Knead until the dough no longer feels sticky and comes away clean from the board. Wash and grease the bowl, return the dough to it, cover and leave until it doubles its bulk.

Turn the dough on to a floured board, flatten to a large round, place the butter, sugar, fruit and peel in the middle and work them in by squeezing and kneading until they are evenly incorporated in the dough. Return the dough again to the greased bowl, cover and leave to rise for 30 minutes.

Divide the dough and shape to fit two 2 lb baking tins. Half fill the tins, cover and leave in a warm place to rise to the top of the tins. Brush with milk. Bake for about 50 minutes in a hot oven (500°, gas mark 10), reducing the heat to 450° (gas mark 8) for the last 15 minutes of baking.

Chelsea buns
¼ pint lukewarm milk (150 ml)
¾ tablespoon dried yeast
1 teaspoon castor sugar
10 oz flour (275g)
½ teaspoon mixed spice
3 oz butter or margarine (75g)
3 oz sugar (75g)
1 egg
4 oz currants (110g)

Dissolve the teaspoon of sugar in some of the liquid and whisk in the yeast. Leave to froth. Sieve the flour with the spice and rub in half the butter. Add half the sugar. Then add the yeast mixture, the beaten egg and the lukewarm milk. Leave in a warm place until it doubles in bulk.

Turn on to a floured board, knead lightly, and roll out to a square. Dot with the remainder of the butter and sprinkle with half the remaining sugar. Fold in three, roll out thinly, and sprinkle with the rest of the sugar and the currants. Roll up like a Swiss roll, cut into 1½ inch slices and place the flat slices close together on a greased warm tin. Leave to prove for 20 minutes. Sprinkle with a little sugar and bake for 20 minutes at 450° (gas mark 8).

Christmas bread

2 tablespoons warm water
½ pint milk (275 ml)
1 teaspoon castor sugar
1 tablespoon dried yeast
1½ lb flour (675g)
1 teaspoon salt
6 oz butter or margarine (175g)
3 eggs
10 oz raisins (275g)
4 oz citron (110g)
1 egg white

Dissolve the teaspoon of castor sugar in warm water. Sprinkle in the yeast and leave to froth. Sift the warmed flour and salt. Make a well in the centre and add the yeast mixture, the melted butter and the beaten eggs, beating well after each addition until the mixture leaves the side of the bowl.

Place in a greased bowl, brush with melted butter, cover and leave in a warm place until it doubles in bulk. Work in the raisins and sliced citron and knead well. Cover and let the mixture rise again until it doubles in bulk. Divide the dough in half and place in greased tins. Brush the tops with egg white, slightly beaten and mixed with 1 tablespoon of water. Bake for 40–50 minutes in a 400° oven (gas mark 6).

Coffee ring

1 tablespoon dried yeast
1 teaspoon castor sugar

¼ **pint lukewarm milk (150 ml)**
1 lb flour (450g)
½ **teaspoon salt**
4 oz butter or margarine (110g)
3 oz castor sugar (75g)
1 egg
1 teaspoon grated lemon rind
4 oz almond paste (110g)
Water icing

Dissolve the teaspoon of castor sugar in the lukewarm milk and whisk in the dried yeast. Leave to froth. Sieve the flour and salt. Cream the butter and gradually add the castor sugar and beat until light and creamy. Add the beaten egg and grated lemon rind. Beat in the yeast mixture, then gradually the sifted flour. Continue beating the dough for 5 minutes. Cover the bowl with a cloth and leave it to rise in a warm place until it has doubled its bulk.

Roll or pat the dough on a greased board into an oblong about ⅓ inch thick. Spread it evenly with almond paste (page 00). Roll as for a Swiss roll and shape the roll into a ring. Place it on a greased baking sheet, cover and leave to rise for 30 minutes. Brush the top with melted butter and sugar or, when roll is baked, give it a topping of water icing. Bake for 40 minutes at 375° (gas mark 5).

Coffee ring (Swedish)

Prepare dough as for the coffee ring. Pat or roll to a 9 × 18 inch oblong. Brush with 2 oz (50g) of melted butter and sprinkle with 4 oz (110g) of raisins, 4 oz of chopped citron, and 3 oz (75g) of sugar, mixed with 1 teaspoon of cinnamon. Roll as for a Swiss roll and form into a ring. Place on a greased sheet. Holding floured scissors perpendicularly, cut bias gashes into the outer edges of the ring, cutting to within an inch of the inner edge. There should be be about 1½ inches between each cut at the outer edge, tapering to ½ inch at the centre. As you cut, turn each partially cut slice flat on the tin. Brush with melted butter and bake for 30 minutes at 375° (gas mark 5).

Croissants

½ tablespoon dried yeast
1 teaspoon castor sugar
½ pint lukewarm milk (275 ml)
1 lb flour (450g)
¼ teaspoon salt
3 oz butter or margarine (75g)
A little beaten egg

Dissolve the sugar in the warm milk and whisk in the yeast; leave to froth. Sieve the flour with the salt. When the yeast mixture is ready, mix with the flour into a dough. Cover and leave in a warm place until the dough doubles in bulk. Roll on a floured board, spread with one-third of the butter, fold in three and seal edges. Repeat rolling and folding twice. Cover and leave for 30 minutes to rise. Roll to ⅛ inch thick, and cut in 5 inch squares. Brush lightly with water. Roll, starting with one corner of each square. Place with top corner underneath

on greased tin. Brush with beaten egg and bake for 12
minutes at 450° (gas mark 8).

Croissants	1 tablespoon dried yeast
(sweet)	1 teaspoon castor sugar
	½ pint lukewarm milk (275 ml)
	1 lb flour (450g)
	4 oz butter or margarine (110g)
	5 oz sugar (150g)
	2 eggs
	3 tablespoons jam
	1 tablespoon chopped almonds

Dissolve the teaspoon of castor sugar in some of the lukewarm
milk and whisk in the yeast. Leave to froth. Sieve the flour and
rub in the butter. Add 4 oz of sugar, the beaten eggs and the
remainder of the milk (retain a little of the egg for a glaze).
Pour in the yeast and mix well together. Roll out to ¼ inch and
cut into 4 inch squares. Put a dab of jam on each square, roll
up and twist into a crescent shape. Place on a greased tin,
brush with beaten egg, and sprinkle with the chopped
almonds and the remainder of the sugar. Leave in a warm
place for 20 minutes, then bake for 20 minutes at 450° (gas
mark 8).

Currant buns	1 tablespoon dried yeast
	1 teaspoon castor sugar
	1½ lb flour (675 ml)
	1 teaspoon salt
	6 oz butter or margarine (175g)
	½ pint of lukewarm milk (275 ml)
	2 oz raisins (50g)
	2 oz currants (50g)
	2 oz candied peel (50g)
	6 oz sugar (175g)

Dissolve the sugar in about ¼ pint of liquid, then whisk in the
yeast and leave to froth. Sift the flour with the salt. Melt the
butter in the lukewarm milk. Add the yeast and milk mixture
to the flour and beat well. Cover and leave in a warm place
until mixture doubles in bulk. Turn on to floured board, mix

in the sugar and fruit and knead well. Cover and leave to rise for 30 minutes. Shape into buns (the recipe makes about 20), place on a greased baking tin and leave in a warm place for 20 minutes. Bake for 15 minutes at 500° (gas mark 10). Just before they are fully cooked, brush with water or egg white and sprinkle with sugar.

Doughnuts

½ tablespoon dried yeast
3 oz castor sugar (75g)
Not quite ¼ pint milk (150 ml)
8 oz flour (225g)
2 oz butter or margarine (50g)
1 beaten egg
Jam

Dissolve 1 teaspoon of the sugar in the lukewarm milk, whisk in the yeast and leave to froth. Sieve the warmed flour and rub the butter into it. Add the beaten egg and 1 oz of sugar. Add the yeast and milk mixture and mix well. Cover and leave in a warm place until the mixture doubles in bulk. Shape into 12 balls, place on a floured tin, cover and leave to rise for 10 minutes. Flatten slightly, place a dab of jam on each and form again into balls. Leave to prove for 10 minutes, then fry for 8 minutes in boiling fat. Drain on kitchen paper and sprinkle with the remainder of the sugar.

Doughnuts (Dutch)

½ tablespoon dried yeast
2 teaspoons castor sugar
½ pint lukewarm milk (275ml)
8 oz flour (225g)
¼ teaspoon salt
Juice of ½ lemon
2 oz currants (50g)
2 oz raisins (50g)
2 oz mixed peel (50g)
1 medium apple

Dissolve the sugar in ¼ pint of the milk. Whisk in the yeast and leave to froth. Prepare the fruit. Sieve the flour with the salt. Make a well in the middle and pour in the yeast mixture.

Add the remainder of the milk and the lemon juice and mix to a dough. Chop the apple finely and add it, the fruit and the peel to the dough and knead well. Shape into a ball, cover and leave in a warm place to rise for 60 minutes. Have a pot of hot oil or fat ready. Drop in small balls of the dough — not too many at a time — and cook until golden brown (about 7 minutes). Drain and sprinkle well with castor sugar.

Durham cake

1 tablespoon dried yeast
1 dessertspoon castor sugar
$\frac{1}{2}$ pint of milk (275g)
1 lb flour (450g)
1 teaspoon mixed spice
$\frac{1}{2}$ teaspoon salt
1 egg
4 oz butter or margarine (110g)
4 oz sugar (110g)
4 oz sultanas (110g)
4 oz currants (110g)
4 oz sliced peel (110g)

Dissolve the sugar in $\frac{1}{4}$ pint of the milk. Whisk in the yeast and leave to froth. Sift the flour with the spice and the salt, and rub in the butter. Make a well in the middle and add the yeast, the well beaten egg and the rest of the milk. Mix to a dough, knead well, cover and leave until it doubles in bulk. Now knead into the dough the creamed butter, sugar, sultanas, currants and sliced peel. Knead well, cover and again leave until it doubles its bulk. Roll out $1\frac{1}{2}$ inch thick, mark the top into small squares with a knife, brush with beaten egg and bake for 45 minutes in a 450° oven (gas mark 8).

Hot cross buns

3 oz sugar (75g)
$\frac{1}{2}$ pint lukewarm milk (275ml)
$\frac{3}{4}$ tablespoon dried yeast
1 teaspoon castor sugar
1 lb flour (450g)
4 oz butter or margarine (110g)
1 egg
1 teaspoon mixed spice

½ **teaspoon salt**
6 oz mixed fruit or currants (175g)
2 oz candied peel (50g)

Dissolve 1 oz of sugar with 1 tablespoon of the milk and set aside for the glaze. Dissolve 1 teaspoon of sugar in some of the milk; whisk in the dried yeast and leave to froth. Sift the flour, salt and spice. Add the sugar, fruit and peel. Make a hollow in the centre and pour in the yeast mixture, the milk, beaten egg and melted butter. Mix to a dough, put on a board and knead, then return to the bowl, cover and leave to double its bulk. Knead again. Form into 16 buns, place on a greased warm tin, and leave to rise for 20 minutes. Mark deeply with a cross, brush with glaze and bake for 15 minutes at 475° (gas mark 9).

Hot cross buns (rich)

1 tablespoon dried yeast
1 teaspoon sugar
½ **pint lukewarm milk (285 ml)**
1½ **lb flour (675g)**
1 teaspoon cinnamon
1 teaspoon ginger
1 teaspoon salt
2 oz sugar (50g)
6 oz butter (175g)
3 eggs
4 oz raisins (110g)
4 oz currants (110g)
4 oz candied peel (110g)
4 oz icing sugar (110g)

Dissolve 1 teaspoon of sugar in ¼ pint of lukewarm milk; whisk in the yeast and leave to froth. Sift the flour, cinnamon, ginger and salt, and add the sugar. Make a hollow in the middle and pour in the yeast mixture, the milk, two beaten eggs and the melted butter. Mix to a dough, turn out on to a floured board and knead for 5–10 minutes. Shape into a ball, place in a lightly greased bowl, cover with a cloth and leave in a warm place until the dough doubles in bulk. Turn on to a floured board and work in the fruit and the peel.

Divide the dough into 24 buns. Flatten them and place

them on a greased baking sheet about 1 inch apart. Make a deep cross in the centre of each. Separate the remaining egg. Brush the buns with the beaten yolk mixed with a little milk and leave them to rise in a warm place until doubled in bulk. Bake for 20 minutes in a 400° oven (gas mark 6). Mix the egg white with the icing sugar and glaze the buns while still warm.

Rum baba	½ tablespoon dried yeast
	1 oz castor sugar (25g)
	¼ pint lukewarm milk (150ml)
	8 oz flour (225g)
	⅛ teaspoon salt
	3 eggs
	4 oz currants (110g)
	4 oz butter or margarine (110g)
	3 tablespoons brown sugar
	2 tablespoons boiling water (30ml)
	1 dessertspoon rum

Dissolve 1 teaspoon castor sugar in the lukewarm milk; whisk in the yeast and leave to froth. Sift the flour and salt and rub in the butter. Make a hollow in the middle and add the yeast mixture, the beaten eggs, the sugar. Mix to a dough, turn on to a floured board and knead. Return to the bowl, cover and leave in a warm place until it doubles in bulk.

Turn on to a floured board and work in the currants. Place the dough in 2 well-greased ring moulds — they should only be one-third full. Cover and leave in a warm place until the dough rises to the top of the tins. Bake for 45 minutes at 400° (gas mark 6). Soak with a syrup made by combining the brown sugar, boiling water and rum.

Sally Lunn	½ tablespoon dried yeast
	1 teaspoon castor sugar
	½ pint lukewarm milk (275 ml)
	12 oz flour (350g)
	½ teaspoon salt
	1 oz butter or margarine (13g)
	1 egg
	1 tablespoon sugar (for glaze)

Dissolve the teaspoon of sugar in ¼ pint of milk; whisk in the yeast and leave to froth. Sieve the flour and salt, and rub in the butter. Make a hollow in the centre and add the yeast mixture, the rest of the milk and the beaten egg. Mix to a dough, turn out on to a floured board and knead. Cover and leave in a warm place to rise. Knead again. Grease well 2 small cake tins, divide the dough between them, and bake for 15 minutes at 450° (gas mark 8) until well browned. Brush with milk, sprinkle with sugar and return to the oven for 5 minutes.

Yorkshire tea cakes

1 tablespoon dried yeast
1 teaspoon castor sugar
¼ pt lukewarm milk (150g)
1 lb flour (450g)
1 teaspoon salt
2 oz lard (50g)
¼ pint boiling water (150 ml)
4 oz currants (110g)
2 oz candied peel (50g)
4 oz sultanas (110g)
Milk and sugar for glaze

Dissolve 1 oz of sugar in the milk; whisk in the yeast and leave to froth. Sift the flour and salt. Make a hollow in the flour and pour in the yeast mixture, the dissolved lard, and mix to a smooth dough. Turn on to a floured board, sprinkle with fruit and knead well. Divide the dough into 6, shape into balls, flatten and pierce with a fork. Place on a greased and floured baking sheet, cover and leave to rise for about 30 minutes in a warm place. Bake for 20 minutes in a hot oven (450°, gas mark 8). Five minutes before they are done, brush with milk and sprinkle with sugar.

Stale bread – too stale for the table – is something which occurs in even the best-regulated kitchens. But those half loaves, heels and despised outside slices need not be consigned to the dustbin. You can crisp them in a cooling oven, crush them with a rolling-pin and store them in dry covered jars for use as coating for fish or cutlets, or as a topping for au gratin dishes.

Cakes

It seems unbelievable that there was a time — and not so very long ago, either — when our village knew nothing of the intricacies of cake-making. Today, if an American visitor were to walk into almost any home in Ballyderrig at tea-time, she would get a surprise in addition to the traditional welcome. Such a surprise, in fact, that she would wonder if she were not back home in Oshkosh or Brooklyn or Quakertown Pa., or in any of the places to which such American delicacies as pineapple upside-down cake and chocolate cookies are indigenous.

It is Polly Sweeney who must be thanked for teaching Ballyderrig to rise above currant bread.

'I'm home to stay,' Polly announced when she came back to us after working for twenty-five years as a cook in the States.

We did not believe her. It was difficult to credit that she would be willing to live in a quiet little place like ours after the grandeur she had known abroad. Polly had certainly grown into a fashionable woman while she was away from us. In church on Sundays, her stylish clothes came between us and our prayers. Ballyderrig seemed to have little to offer such a woman, particularly now that all her own people were dead and gone.

Those who had known her before she went away said that beneath all the style she was the same simple girl who used to keep company with Jimmy Moore, the assistant in Grogan's grocery store.

'Whasn't it luck for her that Jimmy and herself didn't make a match of it?' they said. 'Wasn't it the bright day for her when her people packed her off to America instead of letting her have her way, that time she was so set on marrying him? Look at her now — a well-dressed woman with money in the bank. And look at poor Jimmy, still plodding away in the same old job and not a penny better off than the first day he went to work for Ned Grogan.'

Not, indeed, that anyone who worked for Ned would be likely to make his fortune. Old Ned had a genius for working the last ounce of energy out of a man. And he paid a small grudging wage.

'Polly must be clapping herself on the back for having had such a lucky escape,' was what we all said.

We spoke too soon. The girl was not home more than a month when she and Jimmy were to be seen walking along the bog road in the evenings, holding hands like a pair of children. We noticed that Jimmy had a new firm set to his shoulders, that Polly's face lost the slight hardness it had worn when she first came home, and that her eyes became bright and happy.

She had been back a bare three months when she bought Humpy Hyland's little shop which had stood empty for years. For an exciting couple of weeks we watched contractors from Kildare working early and late as they slapped on snowy paint, fitted gleaming chromium and installed glass-covered shelves. All day long, Polly supervised and directed. In the evening when his day's work for Ned Grogan was through, Jimmy Moore hurried to join Polly and to review the day's progress.

We were not surprised, then, when we heard their banns called. In next to no time, Ned Grogan was looking for a new assistant and Ballyderrig had a second grocery store.

Everyone — excepting, of course, Ned — wished them well, but there were quite a few pessimists who thought that Polly would have been wiser to keep her money in the bank. 'They'll never make a go of it,' said the gloomy prophets. 'Jimmy is one of the decentest fellows in Ireland, but there's no denying that he's a stick-in-the-mud. He's not the type to make a success of a business of his own.'

They reckoned without Polly. She sat in the cash desk while

Jimmy sliced and weighed and wrapped and packaged. There was a go-ahead contented air about him that showed he had at last got what he needed; the one women out of all the world capable of putting life and spirit into him.

But it was not the regeneration of Jimmy that brought custom to the Moores. It was the fact that Polly threw in free with the goods we bought a share of the cooking wisdom she had gathered during her years in America.

'Is that a tin of treacle you are buying?' she would ask. 'You ought to try treacle fruit cake some time.'

Or, 'Would you ever think of making cookies for a change? The children will love them.' And then the recipe would be scribbled out and handed to you with your change.

It was no wonder that old Ned Grogan finally had to put up his shutters. We would have been sorry for him if he had had dependants. But Ned had always been too mean to marry, and there was neither chick nor child to suffer when he retired to an hotel in Newbridge.

'Anyway,' we said, 'why should we have gone on dealing where we got nothing but sour looks and grunts, when the Moores offer us good value, smiles and a free course in cooking?'

Cakes

Here, in one easy lesson, are the simple rules which mean perfection in cake making.

(1) Cream the shortening. Soften it in the mixing bowl with a spoon; and even if the cold weather makes it difficult to cream, don't yield to the temptation of melting it a little. To do this would make the cake greasy and heavy.

(2) For lightness and good texture, add the sugar very gradually, beating well after each addition. The creamed shortening and sugar should be light and fluffy.

(3) The eggs may be beaten or unbeaten, and should be added one at a time; whole eggs if the recipe calls for them, egg yolks alone if the recipe includes stiffly beaten whites. First break each egg into a saucer to make sure it is fresh.

(4) When adding beaten egg whites, fold in gently with an

over-and-over movement until they are completely blended with the mixture.

(5) Add the sifted ingredients (flour, baking powder, salt, spices, etc.) alternately with the milk. Begin and end with the sifted ingredients and fold in rather than beat. Over-beating after the addition of the flour causes a tough cake.

(6) Bake in tins greased preferably with butter. Tins should be two-thirds filled with the mixture.

(7) When baking several layers at once, never place one pan directly over another. Stagger pans in the oven to get the best distribution of heat.

(8) Make sure that the cake is done before you take it from the oven. To test for doneness, open the door just enough to test the cake quickly. Here are a few reliable tests: (a) The cake shrinks from the sides of the pan; (b) It springs back when pressed lightly on top with the finger; if the impression of the finger remains, bake a little longer and test again; (c) A cake-tester or toothpick comes out clean when inserted in the centre of the cake.

(9) Allow the cake to stand in the tin only until it begins to shrink from the sides (about 4 minutes). Then turn out carefully on a wire tray and leave to cool.

(10) To keep fresh, wrap cakes in aluminium foil or grease-proof paper and store in an airtight tin.

'Cakes' is such an enormous category that I have sub-divided it into sections; thereafter recipes are in alphabetical order.

Assorted cakes
Biscuits
Chiffon cakes
Genoese sponge fancies
Gingerbread
Layer cakes
Meringues
Pancakes
Small cakes
Sponge cakes
Fillings and icings

Assorted cakes

Applesauce cake

4 oz butter or margarine (110g)
8 oz castor sugar (225g)
1 egg
12 oz flour (350g)
½ teaspoon salt
1 teaspoon bread soda
2 tablespoons cocoa
1 teaspoon cinnamon
½ teaspoon cloves
8 oz raisins (225g)
4 oz currants (110g)
1 cup sieved sweetened stewed apple

Cream the butter and sugar, and beat in the egg. Sift the flour with the salt, soda, cocoa and the spices, and stir gradually into the creamed mixture. Add the fruit. Beat the stewed apple slightly, and mix it into the batter. Turn into a greased tin and bake for 1½ hours in a moderate oven (350°, gas mark 4).

Banana cake

6 oz flour (175g)
1 teaspoon baking powder
1 teaspoon mixed spice
2 oz butter or margarine (50g)
4 oz castor sugar (110g)
1 egg
2 tablespoons milk (30 ml)
3 large bananas
1 teaspoon cinnamon
1 teaspoon sugar
1 teaspoon coconut

Sift the flour, baking powder and spice twice. Cream the butter and sugar, add the egg and beat well. Add the flour alternately with the milk. Place half the mixture in a greased sandwich tin, spread with the mashed bananas and cover with the remainder of the mixture. Bake for 35 minutes in a 400° oven (gas mark 6). While still hot, spread the top with butter and sprinkle with a mixture of cinnamon, sugar, and coconut.

Buttermilk spice cake

12 oz flour (350g)
3 oz sugar (75g)
$\frac{1}{2}$ teaspoon baking powder
$\frac{3}{4}$ teaspoon bread soda
$\frac{1}{2}$ teaspoon salt
$\frac{1}{2}$ teaspoon cloves
$\frac{1}{2}$ teaspoon cinnamon
2 oz brown sugar (50g)
3 oz butter or margarine (75g)
$\frac{1}{2}$ pint buttermilk (275 ml)
2 eggs

Mix together the flour, sugar, baking powder, bread soda, salt and spices. Add the brown sugar, melted butter and buttermilk, and beat for 2 minutes. Add the eggs and beat for a further 2 minutes. Pour into a greased tin and bake for 50 minutes at 350° (gas mark 4).

Butter sponge

4 oz butter or margarine (110g)
3 oz sugar (75g)
1 teaspoon grated lemon rind
2 eggs
1 tablespoon milk (15 ml)
5 oz flour (150g)
1 teaspoon baking powder

Beat the butter until light. Add the sugar gradually and beat until fluffy. Add the lemon rind, well-beaten eggs and milk, the flour sifted with the baking powder. Turn into a well-greased tin and bake for 45 minutes at 350° (gas mark 4).

Cherry cake (1)

8 oz flour (225g)
$\frac{1}{4}$ teaspoon salt
1 teaspoon baking powder
3 oz washed and dried cherries (75g)
6 oz sugar (175g)
6 oz butter or margarine (175g)
2 eggs
$\frac{1}{2}$ teaspoon vanilla essence
Milk to mix

Sieve the flour, salt and baking powder, and add the quartered cherries. Cream the sugar and butter, beat in the eggs, one by one, and add the vanilla. Add the dry ingredients and barely enough milk to make a stiff mixture. Put into a greased and lined 6 inch tin, place a few halved cherries on top, and bake for 1 hour in a moderate (375°, gas mark 5) oven.

Note: Since it is the melting sugar on cherries which often causes them to sink, washing and drying the fruit thoroughly is important.

Cherry cake (2)

4 oz butter or margarine (110g)
6 oz castor sugar (175g)
3 eggs
12 oz flour (350g)
4 oz sliced citron (110g)
6 oz washed and dried cherries (175g)
1 teaspoon baking powder
¼ teaspoon salt
4 tablespoons cold water (60 ml)

Cream the butter and sugar, and add the unbeaten eggs, one by one, beating well after each addition. Mix about 3 tablespoons of the flour with the citron and the cherries. Sift the remainder of the flour with the baking powder and salt. Add the flour, alternately with cold water, to the creamed mixture, then mix in the fruit. Turn into a tin lined with greased paper and bake for 2¼ hours in a slow oven (325°, gas mark 3).

Chocolate potato cake (rich)

10 oz flour (275g)
½ teaspoon cinnamon
2 teaspoons baking powder
½ teaspoon salt
8 oz butter or margarine (225g)
1 lb castor sugar (450g)
4 eggs
8 tablespoons grated chocolate
5 tablespoons ground almonds
1 cup cold boiled potato
¼ pint milk (150 ml)
1 teaspoon vanilla

Sift the flour, cinnamon, baking powder and salt. Cream the butter with the sugar until light and fluffy. Separate the eggs. Add the yolks, one at a time, to the creamed mixture. Stir in the grated chocolate and the ground almonds. Add the cooked sieved potato. Finally add the flour, alternately with the milk and vanilla, beating gently until smooth after each addition. Whip the egg whites until stiff but not dry. Fold into the cake mixture. Turn into a greased lined tin and bake for 1¾ hours in a moderate oven (350°, gas mark 4).

When cold, cover with chocolate icing (page 121).

Chocolate favourite cake

4 oz flour (110g)
1 oz cornflour (25g)
2 oz grated or powdered chocolate (50g)
1 teaspoon baking powder
4 oz butter or margarine (110g)
4 oz castor sugar (110g)
3 eggs

Sift the flour with the cornflour, chocolate and baking powder. Cream the butter and sugar. Beat the eggs slightly, and add them a little at a time to the creamed mixture. When two-thirds of the eggs are added, add one-third of the flour. Alternate eggs and flour until all are in. Place the mixture in a square-sided tin lined with greased paper, and cook for 45 minutes in a 350° (gas mark 4) oven. When cold, cover top and sides with chocolate icing (page 121).

Make a small amount of butter icing (page 00) and colour it pink. When the chocolate icing is set, pipe pink lines over the top of the cake to form 1 inch squares. In each square place a crystallised violet.

Chocolate fruit cake

6 oz flour (175g)
1 teaspoon baking powder
1 oz cocoa (25g)
4 oz butter or margarine (110g)
4 oz sugar (110g)
2 oz raisins (50g)
2 oz sultanas (50g)

2 eggs
2 tablespoons milk (30 ml)

Sift the flour with the baking powder and cocoa. Cream the butter and sugar. Chop the raisins, and pick over the sultanas. Beat the eggs with the milk. Add the flour, alternately with the eggs and milk, to the creamed mixture. Mix in the fruit. Turn into a well-greased tin and bake for 60 minutes at 350° (gas mark 4).

Christmas cake (rich)

For the caramel:

4 tablespoons sugar
2 tablespoons water

For the cake:

1 lb flour (450g)
Pinch of salt
1 oz mixed spice (25g)
4 oz ground almonds (110g)
1 teaspoon grated lemon rind
4 oz whole almonds (110g)
4 oz washed and dried cherries (110g)
8 oz raisins (225g)
8 oz sultanas (225g)
1½ lb currants (675g)
8 oz chopped peel (225g)
8 eggs
½ glass brandy
2 tablespoons caramel (30ml)
1 dessertspoon orange-flower water
1 dessertspoon rose water
1 lb butter or margarine (450g)
1 lb castor sugar (450g)

To make the caramel, boil 4 tablespoons of sugar and 2 of water in a heavy saucepan over a quick heat until the mixture is a good deep brown. Care must be taken not to let the caramel scorch, as the slightest taste of burning will spoil the flavour of the cake. Use the caramel when cold. (A few drops of lemon juice prevents the mixture from crystallizing).

Sieve together the flour, salt, spices, ground almonds and grated lemon rind. Pour boiling water over the whole almonds, leave them for five minutes, then slip off the skins and shred them finely. Quarter the cherries. Clean the fruit, chop the peel, and combine with the shredded almonds and cherries. Beat the eggs slightly, and add the brandy, caramel, orange-flower water and rose water. Warm the butter slightly in the mixing bowl, but on no account allow it to get oiled. Cut it up and cream with the sugar. Add the eggs, a little at a time, and beat thoroughly but lightly into the creamed mixture. Care must be taken in adding the last of the eggs, or the mixture may curdle, and it is this curdling which gives a cake a coarse pebbly texture. To help to prevent curdling, add a little of the flour mixture before adding the last of the eggs. Now fold in the flour mixture very lightly. Lastly, stir in the fruit.

Prepare a tin (10 inch diagonally by $3\frac{1}{2}$ inch deep) by lining the bottom with two thicknesses of greaseproof paper, and tie a double band of brown paper around the outside of the tin. Stand the tin on a large baking sheet covered with a layer of salt. Put the mixture into the prepared tin, and set it in the middle of the oven. Bake for $5\frac{1}{4}$ hours in a moderately slow oven at 300°–326° (gas mark 2–3).

When baked, allow the cake to stand on the rack for a few minutes, or until it begins to shrink from the sides of the tin. Remove from the tin and place on a cake rack until cold. Store in a cool dry place until about two weeks before Christmas, when the almond icing (page 117) may be put on.

If an extra-rich cake is desired, now and again during the storing period, make a few holes in the top of the cake with a skewer or knitting needle and trickle in a teaspoonful of brandy.

Christmas cake (2)

8 oz butter or margarine (225g)
12 oz sugar (350g)
4 eggs
$1\frac{1}{4}$ lb flour (560g)
1 teaspoon bread soda

½ teaspoon salt
1 teaspoon ground cinnamon
1 teaspoon ground ginger
½ teaspoon ground mace
½ teaspoon ground cloves
½ pint sour milk or sour cream
(275 ml)
8 oz raisins (225g)
8 oz currants (225g)
8 oz sultanas (225g)
8 oz chopped mixed peel (225g)

Cream the butter and gradually add the sugar, creaming well. Add the well-beaten eggs. Sift together the flour, soda, salt and spices, and add to the creamed mixture alternately with the milk. Finally, stir in the fruit and peel. Put into a tin prepared as in the preceding recipe and bake for 3½ hours in a moderately hot oven at 350° (gas mark 4).

Christmas log (1)

5 eggs
6 oz castor sugar (175g)
2 tablespoons water (30ml)
½ teaspoon vanilla
8 oz sifted flour (225g)
¼ teaspoon salt
1 teaspoon baking powder

Separate the eggs. Beat the yolks until very thick and light. Add sugar gradually, beating well after each addition. Add the water and the vanilla, beating in well. Sift together the flour, salt and baking powder. Stiffly beat the egg whites, and add alternately with the flour to the yolk mixture. Line a shallow greased sandwich tin with waxed paper and grease again. Spread the batter evenly and thinly in the tin. Bake in a moderate oven at 350° (gas mark 4) for 20–25 minutes, or until lightly browned.

Turn out immediately on to a damp tea towel. Remove the paper and trim off crusty edges. Spread with apricot jam and roll while still warm. When cool, cover with chocolate icing (page 121).

Christmas log (2)

2 eggs
3 oz castor sugar (75g)
2 oz chocolate (50g)
2 oz flour (50g)
1 teaspoon vanilla

Put the eggs and castor sugar into a bowl, place over hot water and whip for 20 minutes. In the meantime, melt the chocolate in a cup placed in a saucepan containing a little boiling water. Stir the chocolate into the egg mixture, add the flour and vanilla and stir until smooth. Pour into a Swiss roll tin which has been buttered and dusted with flour and castor sugar. Bake for 12–15 minutes in a 425° oven (gas mark 7). Turn on to a towel, roll up loosely and leave until cold. When cold, unroll carefully, spread with cream filling (page 121) and roll again. Coat the roll thickly with icing (page 121).

Cornish cake

⅛ teaspoon salt
⅛ teaspoon cinnamon
⅛ teaspoon nutmeg
¼ teaspoon mixed spice
8 oz flour (225g)
1 oz butter or margarine (25g)
1 oz lard (25g)
2 oz castor sugar (50g)
2 oz currants (50g)
2 oz raisins (50g)
1 oz candied peel (25g)
1 egg
1 tablespoon milk (15ml)

Mix the salt and spices with the flour and rub in the fats. Add the sugar, currants, stoned and chopped raisins and thinly sliced peel. Mix well. Add the well-beaten egg and milk. Turn on to a floured board and form into a flat round cake about 1½ inch thick. Place on a greased baking tin and bake for 25 minutes in a 425° (gas mark 7) oven.

Coconut cake

8 oz flour (225g)
1 teaspoon baking powder
8 oz butter or margarine (225g)
8 oz castor sugar (225g)
2 eggs
2 oz shredded coconut (50g)
2 tablespoons milk (30 ml)
Cochineal

Sift the flour and baking powder. Cream the butter. Add the sugar gradually and beat until light and creamy. Add the egg yolks and beat for 5 minutes. Stir in the coconut and mix well. Gradually add the flour, mixing well. Fold in the stiffly-beaten egg whites, and add enough milk to make a batter that drops easily from the spoon. Add a few drops of cochineal — enough to make the batter a pale pink. Pour into a well-greased tin and bake for 1¼ hours in a 375° (gas mark 5) oven. When cold, cover with coconut icing (page 121).

Date cake

4 oz butter or margarine (110g)
6 oz sugar (175g)
2 eggs
12 oz flour (350g)
1 teaspoon baking powder
¼ teaspoon bread soda
¼ teaspoon salt
2 tablespoons cocoa
1 teaspoon cinnamon
1 teaspoon nutmeg
1½ cups grated raw apple
8 oz chopped stoned dates (225g)

Cream the butter and sugar. Add the eggs, one at a time. Sift the flour with the baking powder, bread soda, salt, cocoa and spices, and add alternately with the grated apple to creamed mixture. Mix in the dates. Turn into a greased tin and bake for 1½ hours at 350° (gas mark 4).

Dundee cake

6 oz sultanas (175g)
3 oz currants (75g)
3 oz candied peel (75g)
3 oz blanched almonds (75g)
9 oz flour (250g)
$\frac{1}{4}$ teaspoon salt
1 teaspoon baking power
6 oz butter or margarine (175g)
6 oz sugar (175g)
3 eggs
Milk to mix

Clean the fruit and slice the peel thinly. Chop the blanched almonds, keeping back about a dozen for the top of the cake. Sieve the flour, salt and baking powder. Cream the butter and sugar and beat in the eggs, one by one. Add the dry ingredients, and mix in barely sufficient milk to make a stiff dropping constency. Place in a greased and lined tin (about 8 inch), and place the halved blanched almonds on top. Bake in a moderate 375° (gas mark 5) oven for $1\frac{1}{2}$–2 hours.

Economy spice cake

$\frac{1}{2}$ pint water (275 ml)
12 oz sultanas (350g)
8 oz brown sugar (225g)
4 oz butter or margarine (110g)
12 oz flour (350g)
1 teaspoon baking powder
1 teaspoon baking soda
1 teaspoon salt
$\frac{1}{2}$ teaspoon cinnamon
$\frac{1}{2}$ teaspoon all spice
$\frac{1}{8}$ teaspoon nutmeg
4 oz chopped candied peel (110g)

Boil together for 3 minutes, the water, sultanas, sugar and butter. Leave until cool. Sift the flour with the baking powder, bread soda, salt and spices. Stir gradually into the cold boiled mixture. Add the finely chopped candied peel. Bake for $1\frac{1}{2}$ hours in a moderate oven at 325° (gas mark 3).

Eggless fruit cake

8 oz sugar (225g)
8 oz fruit (225g)
½ pint water (275 ml)
4 oz clarified dripping (110g)
2 teaspoons mixed spice
12 oz flour (350g)
1 teaspoon bread soda
½ teaspoon baking powder

Boil together for 3 minutes, the sugar, fruit, water, dripping and spice. Sieve the flour with the bread soda and baking powder. Add to the cold boiled mixture and mix well. Bake for 1¾ hours in a moderate oven at 375° (gas mark 5).

Eggless Genoa cake

12 oz flour (350g)
⅛ teaspoon salt
¼ teaspoon cinnamon
¼ teaspoon mixed spice
1 teaspoon baking powder
½ oz cornflour (13g)
8 oz butter or margarine (225g)
6 oz sugar (175g)
1 oz ground almonds (25g)
8 oz raisins (225g)
6 oz sultanas (175g)
4 oz mixed peel (110g)
½ pint milk (275 ml)
1 oz whole almonds (25g)

Sieve the flour with the salt, spices, baking powder and cornflour. Rub in the butter finely. Stir in the sugar, ground almonds, fruit and peel. Mix quickly to a dough with the milk. Turn into a greased and lined tin and place in a moderate oven (350°, gas mark 4) for 2½–3 hours.

About 45 minutes before the cake is done, brush it over with milk and stud it with the whole almonds, blanched and halved.

Fig cake

1 lb dried figs (450g)
¼ pint sour milk (150 ml)
10 oz flour (275g)
1 teaspoon baking powder
1 teaspoon bread soda
1 teaspoon salt
½ teaspoon cinnamon
½ teaspoon ground cloves
¼ teaspoon nutmeg
4 oz butter or margarine (110g)
6 oz sugar (175g)
2 eggs
1 teaspoon vanilla

Simmer the figs until tender in enough water to keep them from burning. Drain and dice them small. Combine ¼ pint of the cold fig juice with the milk. Sift the flour with the baking powder, bread soda, salt and spices. Cream the butter and sugar. Beat in the eggs, one at a time. Add the flour mixture alternately with the milk and the fig juice, beating very gently. Add the vanilla and figs. Bake in a lined greased tin for 1¼ hours in a 350° (gas mark 5) oven.

Fruit cake (light)

9 oz flour (250g)
1 teaspoon baking powder
6 oz butter or margarine (175g)
6 oz castor sugar (175g)
4 eggs
4 oz sultanas (110g)
4 oz raisins (110g)
2 oz candied peel (50g)

Sieve the flour and the baking powder. Cream the butter until light. Gradually add the sugar and beat until light and fluffy. Gradually add the beaten eggs. Mix in half the flour, then the fruit and the chopped peel, then the remainder of the flour. Place in a paper-lined tin (about 7 inch diameter) and bake for about 2 hours in a 325° (gas mark 3) oven.

Fruit cake (spiced)

4 oz raisins (110g)
9 oz flour (250g)
$\frac{1}{2}$ teaspoon cinnamon
$\frac{1}{2}$ teaspoon mixed spice
$\frac{1}{2}$ teaspoon ginger
$1\frac{1}{2}$ teaspoons baking powder
6 oz butter or margarine (175g)
6 oz sugar (175g)
3 eggs
2 oz currants (50g)
1 oz citron peel (25g)
1 oz almonds (25g)
$\frac{1}{4}$ pint milk (150 ml)

Stone and quarter the raisins. Sift the flour, spices and baking powder. Cream the butter; add the sugar and beat until fluffy. Beat the eggs thoroughly, and add alternately with the flour to the creamed mixture. Stir in the fruit, chopped peel and almonds. Add sufficient milk to make a batter that will drop easily from a spoon. Pour into a greased and lined tin and bake for $1\frac{1}{2}$ hours in a 375° (gas mark 4) oven.

Fruit cake (steamed)

12 oz flour (350g)
1 teaspoon bread soda
$\frac{1}{8}$ teaspoon salt
1 teaspoon cinnamon
$\frac{1}{2}$ teaspoon allspice
8 oz sultanas (225g)
4 oz currants (225g)
2 oz halved cherries (50g) — *see page 57*
4 oz chopped mixed peel (110g)
2 oz blanched and chopped almonds
4 oz butter or margarine (110g)
6 oz castor sugar (175g)
4 tablespoons treacle (60 ml)
$\frac{1}{2}$ teaspoon vanilla
3 eggs

Sift the flour, bread soda, salt and spices, and mix with the fruit, peel and blanched almonds. Cream the butter and sugar until light and fluffy. Add the treacle to the creamed mixture, then beat in the vanilla and eggs. Stir in the flour-fruit mixture and blend well, but do not beat. Turn into a greased and lined tin. Tie down with several thicknesses of greased paper and steam for 1 hour; then bake for another $1\frac{1}{2}$ hours in a slow oven at 250 (gas mark $\frac{1}{2}$), removing paper from the top of the tin during the last 15 minutes of baking.

Fruit cake (wholemeal)

4 oz wholemeal flour (110g)
4 oz white flour (110g)
$\frac{1}{8}$ teaspoon salt
$\frac{1}{2}$ teaspoon cinnamon
1 teaspoon baking powder
4 oz butter or margarine (110g)
4 oz sugar (110g)
2 oz ground almonds (50g)
4 oz raisins (100g)
2 oz candied peel (50g)
1 egg
$\frac{1}{4}$ pint milk (150 ml)

Sieve together the wholemeal, white flour, salt, cinnamon and baking powder. Rub in the butter finely. Stir in the sugar, ground almonds, chopped raisins and sliced peel. Mix the beaten egg with the milk and stir it into the dry ingredients. Mix until smooth, turn into a greased tin and bake $1\frac{1}{2}$ hours at 400° (gas mark 6).

Genoa cake

10 oz flour (275g)
$\frac{1}{8}$ teaspoon salt
1 teaspoon baking powder
8 oz butter or margarine (225g)
8 oz castor sugar (225g)
4 eggs
3 oz chopped candied peel (75g)
6 oz sultanas (175g)
2 oz blanched and chopped almonds (50g)
1 teaspoon grated lemon rind

Sift the flour, salt and baking powder. Cream the butter and sugar until light and fluffy. Beat the eggs and add alternately with the flour to the creamed mixture. Add the peel, fruit, nuts and lemon rind. Bake in a shallow greased and lined tin for 1½ hours in a 350° (gas mark 4) oven.

Gold cake

8 oz flour (225g)
1 teaspoon baking powder
¼ teaspoon salt
4 oz butter or margarine (110g)
6 oz sugar (175g)
1 dessertspoon grated orange rind
4 egg yolks
4 tablespoons milk (60 ml)

Sift together the flour, baking powder and salt. Cream the butter until soft and smooth, and gradually add the sugar, beating until very fluffy. Add the orange rind. Beat the egg yolks until very thick and light coloured, and add to the creamed mixture, beating thoroughly. Add the flour alternately with the milk, beating until smooth after each addition. Turn into 3 paper-lined 8 inch sandwich tins and bake for 25–30 minutes in a moderate oven at 375° (gas mark 5). When cool, put the layers together with raspberry jam, and sprinkle the top liberally with castor sugar.

Honey cake

8 oz flour (225g)
⅛ teaspoon salt
¼ teaspoon grated nutmeg
¼ teaspoon powdered cloves
½ teaspoon bread soda
1 teaspoon cream of tartar
3 oz butter or margarine (75g)
4 oz raisins (110g)
2 oz candied peel (50g)
2 tablespoons honey
2 eggs (30 ml)
3 tablespoons milk (45 ml)

Sift together the flour, salt, spices, bread soda, and cream of tartar. Rub in the butter. Stir in the fruit and the sliced peel. Add the honey, the well-beaten eggs and the milk. Turn into a well-greased tin and bake for 1½ hours at 400° (gas mark 6).

Madeira cake

1 lb flour (450g)
1 oz cornflour (25g)
¼ teaspoon salt
2 teaspoons baking powder
5 oz butter or margarine (150g)
8 oz sugar (225g)
3 eggs
1 teaspoon vanilla
¼ pint milk (150 ml)

Sift the flour, cornflour, salt and baking powder. Cream the butter. Add the sugar, one tablespoon at a time, beating well. Add the beaten eggs one at a time, beating well after each addition. Just before beating in the last egg, sprinkle in a little of the flour mixture. Add the vanilla. Fold in the dry ingredients alternately with the milk to the creamed mixture. Bake in a greased lined tin for 1 hour at 350° (gas mark 4).

The Madeira mixture can also be baked in two flat greased tins for 35 minutes in a 375° (gas mark 5) oven, and cut into squares for small fancy cakes. Or bake it in paper cases at 400° (gas mark 6) for 15 minutes.

Variations

Cherry cake
Add 8 oz (225g) of washed and dried cherries to the basic mixture.

Fruit cake
Add 8 oz (225g) of dried fruit and 4 oz (110g) of chopped candied peel, and give the cake another 20 minutes in the oven. Extra additions such as ground almonds, cherries and chopped nuts are up to yourself.

Marble cake
Divide the basic mixture into three. Leave one plain, colour another with a few drops of cochineal, and fold into the third a bar of melted chocolate. Put the mixture in alternate dollops into the tin, and bake as usual.

Seed cake
Add a dessertspoon of caraway seeds to the basic mixture.

Small cake ideas:
Brush with hot jam and roll in chopped nuts or shredded coconut. Cover with marzipan. Coat with butter icing. Dip in fondant. Split and sandwich a dab of jam and whipped cream between the halves. Cut the squares large and pile with crushed sweetened fruit and cream.

Marmalade cake

1 lb flour (450g)
¼ teaspoon salt
½ teaspoon bread soda
1 teaspoon baking powder
4 oz butter or margarine (110g)
6 oz sugar (175g)
2 eggs
4 tablespoons orange marmalade

Sift the flour, salt, soda and baking powder. Cream the butter, add the sugar gradually and beat until light and fluffy. Beat in the eggs. Mix in the dry ingredients, then add the marmalade. Turn into a greased and floured tin and bake for 50 minutes at 350° (gas mark 4). Turn out of the tin immediately it is cooked or it may stick.

This mixture also makes very nice biscuits. Drop in spoonfuls on a greased tin about 2 inch apart, and bake for 12 minutes in a moderate oven. Remove immediately from tin when cooked.

Porter cake

1 lb flour (450g)
¼ teaspoon salt
1 teaspoon baking powder
8 oz sugar (225g)
½ teaspoon nutmeg
½ teaspoon mixed spice
8 oz butter or margarine (110g)
1 lb sultanas (450g)
2 oz chopped peel (150g)
½ pint porter or stout (275 ml)
2 eggs

Sieve the flour, salt and baking powder, and add the sugar, nutmeg and spice. Rub in the butter finely. Add the fruit, then the porter which has been mixed with the beaten eggs. Bake in a well-greased tin for 2½ hours at 350° (gas mark 4).

Prune cake

6 oz butter or margarine (175g)
8 oz castor sugar (225g)
2 eggs
1 cup of prune pulp (stewed and sieved prunes)
10 oz flour (275g)
1½ teaspoons of bread soda
½ teaspoon salt
1 teaspoon cinnamon
¾ teaspoon ground cloves
¼ pint sour milk or buttermilk (150 ml)

Cream the butter and sugar. Beat in the eggs, one at a time, and then the prune pulp. Sift the flour with the bread soda, salt and spices. Add to the creamed mixture alternately with the sour milk. Bake for about 1 hour in a 350° oven (gas mark 4). Or bake in two greased sandwich tins for 30 minutes in a 375° oven (gas mark 5), and put the layers together when cool with butter cream (page 119).

Raisin cake

¼ teaspoon saffron
12 oz flour (350g)
⅛ teaspoon salt
1½ teaspoons baking powder
3 oz butter or margarine (75g)
3 oz brown sugar (75g)
1 egg
¼ pint milk (150 ml)
4 oz raisins (110g)
4 oz currants (110g)

Put the saffron in a cup and cover with a tablespoon of water. Leave for about 1 hour before using. Sift the flour, salt and baking powder. Cream the butter and sugar. Combine the beaten egg with the liquid from the saffron and the milk. Add, alternately with the flour, to the creamed mixture. Stir in the fruit. Bake for about 1¾ hours at 375° (gas mark 5).

Simnel cakes

Mothering Sunday, the mid-Sunday of Lent, calls for a special cake for mothers, a pleasant custom which dates from Elizabethan times. In those days, girls who had hired themselves as servants at the New Year were given a holiday in mid-Lent so that they might visit their families. To prove their cooking skill, they brought home a gift of a 'Mothering' or 'Simnel' cake. And because the Lenten fast in those times was rigorous, they used a rich mixture so that the cake would keep until Easter.

As well as this evidence of her newly acquired cooking skill, the girl sometimes brought home for family approval her newly acquired sweetheart. And, if she happened to be a dairymaid or laundry maid, the sweetheart bought or had made for her the simnel cake. There is an old verse which goes:

> *And I'll to thee a simnel bring*
> *'Gainst thou goest a-mothering;*
> *So that when she blesses thee*
> *Half the blessing thou'lst give me.*

Recipe 1 (rich)

8 oz flour (225g)
½ teaspoon grated nutmeg
½ teaspoon ground cinnamon
½ teaspoon ground ginger
¼ teaspoon salt
1 teaspoon baking powder
8 oz butter (225g)
8 oz castor sugar (225g)
12 oz cleaned and prepared sultanas (350g)
12 oz currants (350g)
4 oz washed and dried cherries (110g)
4 oz chopped peel (110g)
4 eggs
1 tablespoon milk (15 ml)
1 teaspoon vanilla
Almond paste

Sift together the flour, grated nutmeg, ground cinnamon, ground ginger, salt and baking powder. Cream the butter and the sugar. Beat the eggs, add the milk and vanilla and work into the creamed mixture. Gradually add half the flour, then add all the fruit, and finally mix in the remainder of the flour. (The cake mixture should be fairly stiff.)

Line a 9 inch tin with several thicknesses of greaseproof paper. Put half the mixture into the tin, smoothing the top evenly. Over this place a layer of almond paste (page 117). Add remainder of the mixture and smooth the top. Bake in a slow oven (325°, gas mark 3) for 4 hours.

When the cake is cool, cut out another round of almond paste exactly the size of the cake, cutting out a 3 inch round from the centre. Lay the ring of paste on the top of the cake. Form a number of small balls or eggs (11 is the traditional number) with the remainder of the paste and put these at intervals on the almond-paste ring. Brush with beaten egg, and place in a hot oven (475°, gas mark 9) for 3 minutes or until the paste is slightly brown. When cold, fill the centre gap with glacé icing, and, when this is set, pipe an appropriate inscription — *To Mother* — or whatever you please.

Recipe 2

5 oz flour (150g)
¼ teaspoon nutmeg
¼ teaspoon cinnamon
1 teaspoon baking powder
¼ teaspoon salt
3 oz butter or margarine (75)
3 oz castor sugar
1 large or 2 small eggs
2 tablespoons milk (30 ml)
1 oz chopped peel (25g)
4 oz raisins (110g)
4 oz sultanas (110g)
1 lb almond paste (450g)

Sift together the flour, nutmeg, cinnamon, baking powder and salt. Cream the butter with the sugar. Beat the eggs, mix in the milk, and add, alternately with the flour, to creamed mixture. Mix in the fruit. Divide the mixture. Put half in a greased, lined 5 inch tin, smooth the top and over it place a layer of almond paste. Add the remainder of the cake mixture, smooth evenly and bake for 2½ hours in a moderate oven (350°, gas mark 4). Finish cake as in the preceding recipe.

Biscuits

Americans call them cookies. One of the finest institutions of family life there is the cookie jar into which the junior members of the family may dip when hunger or their good behaviour warrants the treat.

Too much flour used in the rolling of biscuits will spoil their appearance and taste. It is a good idea, therefore, to roll the dough between sheets of waxed paper. As the dough should be very thin, it is sometimes difficult to lift the cut-out cookies on to the baking sheet. A spatula or fish slice may be used. A better idea still is to roll the dough on the bottom of an inverted greased and lightly floured baking sheet. Cut the dough into shapes and remove the surplus dough between the cookies. To keep the cookies from sticking, use unsalted fat (such as lard). Or, cover the sheet with greased paper.

Almond biscuits

3 oz butter or margarine (75g)
3 oz castor sugar (75g)
6 oz flour 175g)
1 egg

Cream the butter and sugar, then add the flour. Mix well. Stir in enough beaten egg to make a soft but firm dough. Roll out very thinly, cut into circular shapes, and bake for 15 minutes at 350° (gas mark 4).

Make an almond topping as follows: Blanch and chop 1 oz (25g) almonds. Mix with 4 oz (110g) of castor sugar and the grated rind of ½ lemon. Beat two egg whites stiffly and mix with the almond mixture. When the cut out biscuits are placed on the baking sheet, put a small amount of the almond mixture on each and bake for 12 minutes at 375° (gas mark 5).

Brownies

4 oz butter or margarine (110g)
6 oz brown sugar (175g)
1 egg
¼ pint milk (150 ml)
1 teaspoon vanilla
6 oz flour (175g)
1½ oz cocoa (40g)
1 teaspoon baking powder
½ teaspoon salt
6 oz flakemeal (175g)

Cream the butter and the sugar. Combine the beaten egg, milk and vanilla. Sift together the flour, cocoa, baking powder and salt. Add to the creamed mixture, alternately with the egg and milk. Fold in the flakemeal. Drop in tablespoons on a greased baking sheet and cook for 12–15 minutes in a hot oven (400° gas mark 6).

Caraway biscuits

4 oz butter or margarine (110g)
12 oz flour (350g)
4 oz castor sugar (110g)
½ teaspoon caraway seeds

Rub the butter into the flour until the mixture looks like fine breadcrumbs. Stir in the sugar until evenly mixed, and then add the caraway seeds. Mix to a stiff dough with cold water. Roll out very thinly, cut in rounds and diamonds and bake for 15 minutes at 375° (gas mark 5).

Chankele (Christmas candles)

3 eggs
5 oz icing sugar (150g)
6 oz ground almonds (175g)
4 oz flour (110g)

Beat the eggs until light. Add the sugar gradually and beat until thick. Stir in the almonds and enough flour to make a soft dough. Turn dough on to a floured board and form into little rolls the shape of a very small candle. Fry in deep hot fat for 2 minutes or until golden brown. Drain, cool and roll in more icing sugar.

Chilled cookies

4 oz butter or margarine (110g)
4 oz white sugar (110g)
4 oz brown sugar (110g)
2 eggs
1 teaspoon vanilla
12 oz flour (350g)
1 teaspoon baking powder
¼ teaspoon salt
3 oz chopped walnuts (75g)

Cream the butter, then beat in the sugar gradually. Beat in the eggs one at a time, and continue beating until light. Add the vanilla, then the flour which has been sifted with the baking powder and salt. Add the walnuts and form dough into 2 firm rolls. Leave in the fridge or a very cold place for 24 hours. Cut into very thin slices and bake for 10 minutes at 400° (gas mark 6).

Christmas biscuits

8 oz flour (225g)
1 teaspoon baking powder
8 oz castor sugar (225g)
4 oz butter (110g)
2 egg yolks
1 teaspoon vanilla
2 egg whites
2 oz chopped nuts (50g)

Sift together the flour, baking powder and sugar. Cut in the butter finely. Stir in the egg yolks and vanilla, and work dough until smooth. Leave in a cold place for a couple of hours until firm. Roll thinly on a lightly floured board and cut as desired. Brush with egg white and sprinkle with chopped nuts. Bake on an ungreased baking sheet for 10–12 minutes in a 375° oven (gas mark 5).

Christmas drop cakes

6 oz flour (175g)
1 teaspoon baking powder
8 oz butter or margarine (225g)
8 oz sugar (225g)
3 eggs

Rind and juice of $\frac{1}{2}$ **lemon**
$\frac{1}{8}$ **teaspoon salt**
4 oz currants (110g)

Sift the flour and baking powder. Work the butter and sugar to a smooth cream, then slowly beat in the whole eggs, one at a time. Add a little of the flour, the lemon rind and juice and the salt. Slowly beat in the rest of the flour, then the currants (which have been mixed with some of the flour). Drop the mixture by spoonfuls on a very well greased baking sheet, leaving plenty of room to spread. Bake for 10–12 minutes in a moderate oven (350°, gas mark 4).

Christmas
shortbread

8 oz butter or margarine (225g)
8 oz icing sugar (225g)
1 lb flour (450g)
1 teaspoon baking powder

Cream the butter, beating in the sieved icing sugar. Gradually work in the flour which has been sieved with the baking powder. Knead well, roll out about $\frac{1}{4}$ inch thick and cut in strips about 2×3 inch. Bake for 45 minutes in a 300° oven (gas mark 2), taking care not to brown the shortbread. When cooked, coat each piece of shortbread evenly with icing sugar.

Christmas
stars

4 oz butter or margarine (110g)
3 oz castor sugar (75g)
3 egg yolks
2 tablespoons cream (30 ml)
8 oz flour (225g)
1 tablespoon water (15 ml)
4 oz icing sugar (110g)
4 oz whole almonds (110g)

Cream the butter with all but 1 tablespoon of the sugar. Beat in egg yolks and the cream. Gradually stir in the flour (except for 1 tablespoon) until the dough is just stiff enough to roll. Leave in the fridge or a cold place to get firm. Sprinkle the baking board with the remaining tablespoon of sugar mixed with 1 tablespoon of flour. Place the dough on this and roll ¼ inch thick. Cut with a star-shaped cutter, lift with a fish slice and place on an ungreased baking sheet. Bake for 15–20 minutes in a 350° oven (gas mark 4). When cold, spread with icing made by mixing the remaining egg yolk with the water and icing sugar. Blanch and chop the almonds and scatter over the iced biscuits before the icing dries.

Coconut biscuits

6 oz flour (175g)
½ teaspoon salt
3 oz butter or margarine (75g)
1 tablespoon golden syrup (15 ml)
¾ teaspoon bread soda
2 tablespoons boiling water (30 ml)
4 oz shredded coconut (110g)
4 oz flake oatmeal (110g)
6 oz sugar (175g)
1 teaspoon vanilla

Sift the flour and salt. Melt the butter with the golden syrup. Dissolve the soda in boiling water, and mix all the ingredients together. Drop in dessertspoons on a greased baking sheet, leaving room for spreading. Bake for about 15 minutes in a 350° oven (gas mark 4). Lift off with a spatula.

Coconut chews

2 oz butter or margarine (50g)
4 oz brown sugar (110g)
1 egg
1 teaspoon vanilla
4 oz flour (110g)
1 teaspoon baking powder
½ teaspoon salt
3 oz grated coconut (75g)

Melt the butter in a saucepan and stir in the sugar until dissolved. Cool slightly, then beat in the egg and vanilla. Sift the dry ingredients and add. Finally stir in the coconut. Pour the butter into a greased and floured pan, 8×8 inch. Bake for 30 minutes in a 350° oven (gas mark 4). When cold, cut in bars and roll in icing sugar.

Date bars

3 eggs
6 oz castor sugar (175g)
4 oz chopped dates (110g)
1 teaspoon vanilla
6 oz flour (175g)
1 teaspoon baking powder
½ teaspoon salt
¼ teaspoon ground cloves
¼ teaspoon cinnamon

Beat the eggs until light. Add the sugar gradually and beat until very light and creamy. Add the chopped dates and vanilla. Sift together the dry ingredients and add gradually, beating lightly until well blended. Pour into a greased and floured baking tin, 9×13 inch. Bake for 30 minutes at 350° (gas mark 4). When cold, cut in bars and roll in icing sugar.

Date crunchies

1 lb flour (450g)
1 teaspoon baking powder
½ teaspoon salt
6 oz flakemeal (175 ml)
8 oz brown sugar (225g)
3 oz butter or margarine (75g)
3 oz lard (75g)
A little milk

Sift together the flour, baking powder and salt. Add the flakemeal and sugar, and mix thoroughly. Beat in the melted butter and lard. Add sufficient milk to make a stiff dough. Roll out thinly, cut in small rounds and bake for about 15 minutes in a 375° oven (gas mark 5). When cold put two biscuits together with date filling (page 123).

Date honey bars

3 eggs
6 tablespoons honey (90 ml)
8 oz flour (225g)
½ teaspoon salt
1 teaspoon baking powder
4 oz chopped dates (110g)
2 oz chopped nuts (50g)

Beat the eggs well and gradually beat in the honey. Sift the dry ingredients, then stir in. Add the dates and nuts. Place the batter in a greased and floured tin, 9×13 inch. Bake for about 30 minutes at 350° (gas mark 4). When cool, cut in bars.

Easter biscuits

8 oz butter or margarine (225g)
8 oz castor sugar (225g)
½ teaspoon almond extract
2 egg yolks
14 oz flour (400g)
½ teaspoon salt
1 egg white

Cream the butter until light and gradually beat in the sugar. Add the almond extract which has been mixed with the beaten egg yolks. Gradually stir in the flour sifted with the salt, and leave in a cold place for about 2 hours. Roll out thinly, and cut in rounds. Brush with egg white beaten with 1 teaspoon of water. Sprinkle with coarse sugar and bake for 8 minutes at 400° (gas mark 6).

Fruit bars

3 eggs
4 oz brown sugar (110g)
5 oz flour (150g)
½ teaspoon baking powder
½ teaspoon all spice
½ teaspoon ground cloves
1 teaspoon cinnamon
4 oz sultanas (110g)
8 oz chopped figs, dates or prunes (225g)

Beat the eggs until light. Beat in the brown sugar gradually. Sprinkle about a tablespoon of the flour over the fruit and distribute it evenly. Sift the rest of the flour with the spices and stir into the egg mixture. Stir in the fruit. Pour into a greased and floured tin and bake for 25 minutes in a 350° oven (gas mark 4). When cool, cut in bars and roll in icing sugar.

(If dried prunes or figs are used, they should be steamed until soft. Or soak them in water until soft; then dry.)

Fruit crisps

8 oz flour (225g)
1 teaspoon baking powder
½ teaspoon salt
6 oz flakemeal (175g)
4 oz sultanas (110g)
4 oz brown sugar (110g)
1 egg
2 tablespoons treacle (30 ml)
2 tablespoons apricot jam
4 oz butter or margarine (110g)

Sift the flour, baking powder and salt. Add the flakemeal and sultanas. Combine the sugar and egg, and beat into this mixture the treacle, jam and melted butter. Stir into the flour mixture. Drop by tablespoons on a greased baking sheet and cook for 15 minutes at 375° (gas mark 5).

Halloween witches

12 oz flour (350g)
½ teaspoon salt
1 teaspoon baking powder
6 oz butter or margarine (175g)
4 oz castor sugar (110g)
1 egg
Milk for mixing

Cut the outline of a witch in firm cardboard for a pattern. Sift the flour with the salt and baking powder. Rub in the butter finely. Add the sugar and the lightly beaten egg and mix to a very stiff dough with the milk. Roll out about ⅛ inch thick. Fold the dough in four and place the cardboard pattern on it. Cut around the outline with a sharp knife. With a fish slice, lift each 'witch' on to a greased baking sheet. Add currants for eyes. Bake for about 12 minutes at 375° (gas mark 5) until golden brown. When cold, pipe on belt, hat, etc. with chocolate icing.

Honey chews

4 oz butter or margarine (110g)
8 oz sugar (225g)
2 tablespoons honey
¼ teaspoon salt
2 eggs

$\frac{1}{2}$ **teaspoon vanilla**
10 oz flour (275g)
1 teaspoon baking powder

Beat the butter until soft. Add the sugar gradually and beat until light and fluffy. Add the honey and salt. Beat in the eggs, one at a time. Add the vanilla. Sift the flour with the baking powder and stir into the creamed mixture. Drop the batter, a dessertspoon at a time, on to a greased sheet, allowing room for spreading. Decorate each biscuit with a nut, a raisin, or some crystallized cherry. Bake at 400 ° (gas mark 6) for about 12 minutes.

Honey lace crisps

6 oz flour (175g)
$\frac{1}{4}$ **teaspoon salt**
4 oz castor sugar (110g)
4 tablespoons honey (60 ml)
2 oz butter or margarine (50g)
$\frac{1}{2}$ **teaspoon vanilla**

Sift the flour and salt. Add the castor sugar. Heat the strained honey in a medium size saucepan almost to boiling point, then add the butter and stir until melted. Add the vanilla. Stir in the dry ingredients and mix well (the batter should be thin). Drop by tablespoons on a well-buttered baking sheet about 4 inch apart. Bake in a moderate oven at 375° (gas mark 5) for 6–8 minutes or until golden brown. Cool for a minute, then remove with a spatula and shape over a small glass or jar turned upside down to make little shells with flaring rims. Leave until hard, then remove and cool. (If they become too brittle to shape easily, return to oven for a minute to soften.)

Kringles

8 oz flour (225g)
1 teaspoon baking powder
$\frac{1}{4}$ **teaspoon salt**
4 oz butter or margarine (110g)
8 oz sugar (225g)
2 eggs
2 teaspoons caraway seeds
2 tablespoons brandy (30 ml)
4 oz icing sugar (100g)

Sift 6 oz of flour with the baking powder and salt. Cream the butter and sugar, and beat in the eggs, caraway seeds and brandy. Stir in the flour mixture, then add the rest of the flour until the dough is stiff enough to handle. Leave in a cold place until firm. Roll ⅛ inch thick on a lightly floured board, cut in desired shapes, place on an ungreased baking sheet and sprinkle with icing sugar. Bake in a 375° (gas mark 5) for 10–15 minutes.

Lemon biscuits

Make dough as for almond biscuits (page 67), adding 1 teaspoon of lemon rind to the basic recipe. When the biscuits are baked, beat the white of an egg to a stiff froth and add enough castor sugar to thicken. Brush the cold biscuits with this and leave to dry.

Oatcakes

4 oz flakemeal (110g)
4 oz ground oats (110g)
¾ teaspoon salt
1 oz lard (25g)
Hot water to mix

Mix together the flakemeal, oats and salt. Rub in the lard. Add sufficient hot water to make a stiff dough. Knead lightly for a minute or two, then turn out on a board dusted with ground oats. Divide into three parts. Roll each piece to a round and cut in quarters. Bake for 20–25 minutes in a slow oven (325°, gas mark 3), turning the cakes after 15 minutes. Or you can cook them in a heavy pan on top of the of the stove. When the cakes are cooked, stand them in a warm place to become thoroughly dry and crisp.

Oatmeal macaroons

6 oz flakemeal (175g)
½ teaspoon salt
2 oz castor sugar (50)
2 oz butter or margarine (50g)
1 small egg

Mix the flakemeal with the salt, sugar and melted butter. Add enough beaten egg to make a light and crumbly mixture. Fill a tablespoon with the mixture, level it against the side of the bowl, and with the aid of a knife unmould on to a greased baking sheet. Bake for 20 minutes at 357° (gas mark 5), or until crisp and lightly browned.

Savoy fingers

3 eggs
5 oz castor sugar (150g)
5 oz flour (150g)

Beat the eggs and sugar over hot water until light coloured and so thick that the mixture holds traces of the whisk. Gradually fold in the sifted flour. Place a meringue tube in a forcing bag, turn back the top of the bag and three-quarters fill with the mixture. Now fold over the top of the bag and use it as for icing. To get the Savoys the same size, fold kitchen paper in 3½ inch bands; unfold them and place on the baking sheet. Pipe the fingers on to the paper, 3½ inch long and ½ inch apart, keeping all the same length by following the folds of the paper. Sieve castor sugar over the fingers, then lift up the edge of the paper and shake off the excess sugar. Bake in a 450° oven (gas mark 8) for about 4 minutes. To remove from the paper, brush the back of the paper with water — it should then pull away easily.

Shortbread

1 lb flour (450g)
2 oz cornflour (50g)
5 oz castor sugar (150g)
10 oz butter (275g)

Sift the flour and cornflour, and add the sugar. Warm the butter slightly and rub into the flour. Work together until smooth and malleable. Divide into three parts and press into three greased sandwich tins, smoothing the top with a knife. Bake for 40 minutes at 350° (gas mark 4). Sprinkle with castor sugar and cut into triangles while hot.

Sugar fingers

6 oz butter or margarine (175g)
4 oz castor sugar (110g)
1 egg
12 oz flour (350g)
1 teaspoon baking powder
1 teaspoon vanilla (or ½ teaspoon grated lemon rind)

Cream the butter and sugar. Add the beaten egg. Sift in the flour and baking powder, and add the vanilla. Turn on to a floured board, roll thinly, brush with beaten egg and sprinkle with sugar. Cut into fingers and place on a greased baking sheet. Bake for 12 minutes at 400° (gas mark 6).

Treacle bars

3 oz butter or margarine (175g)
1½ oz castor sugar (40g)
1 egg
3 tablespoons treacle (45 ml)
⅛ teaspoon salt
⅛ teaspoon bread soda
2 oz flour (50g)
1 teaspoon vanilla
4 tablespoons chopped nuts

Beat the butter until soft. Add the sugar gradually and beat until light and creamy. Beat in the egg, treacle, salt and bread soda. Add the flour in 3 parts to the butter mixture. Stir in the vanilla and beat the batter until smooth. Stir in the nuts and/or raisins. Bake in a greased 8×8 inch tin at 375° (gas mark 5) for about 15 minutes. Cut the cake into bars before it is cold. Roll the bars in castor sugar.

Treacle double-deckers

12 oz flour (350g)
1 teaspoon salt
1 teaspoon baking powder
¾ teaspoon bread soda
2 teaspoons ginger
4 oz butter or margarine (110g)
6 oz sugar (175g)
2 eggs
4 tablespoons treacle (60 ml)
3 tablespoons boiling water (45 ml)

Sift together the dry ingredients. Cream the butter and sugar, and add the well-beaten eggs and treacle. Mix well, and add the flour mixture alternately with the water. When well mixed, roll out thinly on a lightly floured board (about ⅛ inch thick). Cut in small rounds. Bake at 350° (gas mark 4) for 8–10 minutes. When cool put together with any creamy filling, or with butter icing.

Vanilla biscuits

2 oz lard (50g)
2 oz butter or margarine (50g)
3 oz castor sugar (75g)
4 oz flour (110g)
¼ teaspoon bread soda
1 teaspoon baking powder
¼ teaspoon salt
1 teaspoon golden syrup
3 teaspoons boiling water
1 egg
1 teaspoon vanilla
4 oz flakemeal (110g)

Cream the lard, butter and sugar together until light and fluffy. Sift the flour, bread soda, baking powder and salt. Blend the golden syrup with the boiling water and combine with the beaten egg and vanilla. Add alternately with the flour to the creamed mixture. Fold in the flakemeal. Roll out thinly on a floured board. Cut in rounds. Bake on a greased baking sheet for 12–15 minutes at 375° (gas mark 5) or until golden brown. When cool, put together with custard or coffee filling (pages 122, 123).

Chiffon cakes

The success of this cake depends on the stiffness of the egg whites, so they should be beaten until they are really stiff.

A special 'tube' tin is used for baking, with a funnel up the centre. This means that the cake has a circular hole in the middle. When baked, remove from the oven and immediately invert over a funnel or bottle, letting the cake hang free while cooling. Unless this precaution is taken, the cake will be soggy and will be impossible to remove from the tin.

When the cake is cold, loosen around the sides with a spatula. Then turn the tin upside down and knock sharply against the table — the cake will then drop out.

Chiffon cakes may also be cooked in ordinary oblong tins (13×9×2 inch). In this case, when the cake is baked, turn the tin upside down and rest the edges on two other tins so that the cake hangs free while cooling.

Basic recipe

18 oz flour (500g)
12 oz castor sugar (350g)
1 teaspoon baking powder
1 teaspoon salt
8 tablespoons salad oil (120 ml)
5 egg yolks
6 tablespoons cold water (90 ml)
1 teaspoon vanilla
2 teaspoons grated lemon rind
7 egg whites
$\frac{1}{2}$ teaspoon cream of tartar

Sift together the flour, sugar, baking powder and salt. Make a well in the centre and add in this order — the salad oil, unbeaten egg yolks, water, vanilla and lemon rind. Beat until smooth. Put the egg whites into a large bowl and sprinkle with cream of tartar. Beat until they are stiff and dry. Take the bowl of egg yolk mixture in one hand and a spatula in the other, and add the mixture very gradually, folding it into the whites carefully and gently. Pour immediately into an ungreased tube pan (10×4) inch and bake at 325° (gas mark 4) for another 10–15 minutes, or until the top springs back when touched.

Cherry chiffon cake
Drain 3 oz (75g) of marashino cherries and chop them finely. Use the basic recipe but substitute 3 tablespoons of liquid from the cherries for 3 tablespoons of water. Omit the lemon rind and use only ½ teaspoon of vanilla. When the batter is made, fold the cherries in gently. Ice with white icing (page 128) and decorate with cherry halves.

Orange chiffon cake
Substitute 6 tablespoons of orange juice for the 6 tablespoons of cold water. Omit the vanilla and lemon rind and use instead 1 tablespoon of orange rind. Ice with orange icing (page 125).

Pineapple chiffon cake
Substitute 6 tablespoons of pineapple syrup from tinned pineapple or pineapple juice instead of the 6 tablespoons of water. Omit the vanilla. Cover with pineapple icing (page 126).

Spice chiffon cake
Add to the dry ingredients, 1 teaspoon cinnamon and ½ teaspoon each of nutmeg, cloves, allspice and ginger. Ice with chocolate icing (page 121).

Genoese sponge fancies

A Genoese sponge is the ideal mixture from which to make an assortment of fancy cakes. When cooked and cool, the sponge may be cut into rounds, diamonds and squares, and decorated to taste.

Basic recipe

7 oz flour (200g)
1 teaspoon baking powder
1 oz cornflour (25g)
4 eggs
8 oz castor sugar (225g)
4 oz butter or margarine (100g)

Line two shallow baking tins measuring 9×12 inch with well-buttered greaseproof paper, and sprinkle the paper with about 2 desertspoons of the flour. Sift the remaining flour with the baking powder and the cornflour. Beat the eggs over hot water, add the sugar and beat well until the mixture is light and thick enough to hold a trace of the egg-beater. Fold in the sieved flour evenly and lightly. Heat the butter sufficiently to melt it (but do not let it become oily) and fold lightly into the flour mixture. Divide the mixture between the two tins and bake for 20 minutes in a hot oven (400°, gas mark 6). It should be golden brown all over and resilient to the touch.

Some suggestions for using Genoese sponge

Almond bars
Brush a long piece of sponge with warm apricot jam. Place a layer of marzipan along the top of the sponge. Cut into 2-inch lengths and coat with white icing (page 128).

Cauliflowers
Colour marzipan green, roll out very thinly and cut into 'leaves'. Cut the sponge into rounds, and brush the sides with warm apricot jam. Fix 3 leaves around each little cake to cover the sides completely. Fill the top with white icing (page 128).

Cherry cakes
Cut squares of the sponge. Spread the tops and sides with white icing (page 128) and place a cherry on each.

Chocolate baskets

Melt a couple of bars of chocolate and pour into a shallow greased tin to set in a thin sheet. With a sharp knife, cut it into pieces to fit the sides of small squares of Genoese sponge. Brush the cakes with warmed apricot jam, top and sides, and stick a piece of chocolate to each side. Cover the top with whipped cream or with shredded coconut.

Coffee cakes

Spread diamonds of Genoese sponge with coffee icing (page 122) and place a halved walnut on each.

Dominoes

Cut Genoese sponge in oblongs, split, spread with raspberry jam and put together again. Spread with white icing (page 128). When the icing is set colour additional icing with chocolate (mix a little cocoa and white icing). Pipe two lines close together across the cake to divide the domino, then pipe dots on each side. Make a different number of dots on each domino.

Hedgehogs

Cut rounds of Genoese sponge, spread all over with raspberry or apricot jam and roll in shredded coconut.

Lemon diamonds

With a warm knife, spread lemon icing on diamonds of Genoese sponge. In the centre of each, place a sliver of candied lemon peel.

Orange cream cakes

Split squares of Genoese sponge and spread with orange butter cream (page 119). Put together and sift fine castor sugar on top.

Orange fingers

Split fingers of Genoese sponge and spread with marmalade. Cover with orange icing (page 125).

Raspberry fingers

Split fingers of Genoese sponge and spread with raspberry jam. Pour warm lemon icing (page 124) gently over the cakes.

Violettes
Cover the top and sides of squares of Genoese sponge with chocolate icing (page 121) and place a crystallized violet on top of each.

Gingerbread

Small wonder that Hansel and Gretel were beguiled by that gingerbread house. There never lived a child who could resist the spicy sweetness of fresh gingerbread. And its allure is not confined to the younger members of the family. With a sweet-tooth of any age this easy-to-make, easy-on-the-purse cake is a steady favourite. As well as being a tea-time favourite, ginger-bread can be a wonderful dessert. No sauce is needed. But for extra special occasions, just try hot gingerbread with vanilla or lemon sauce, or with vanilla ice cream.

*Everyday
gingerbread*

1 egg
4 oz brown sugar (110g)
8 tablespoons treacle (120 ml)
4 oz butter or margarine (110g)
¼ pint hot water (150 ml)
12 oz flour (350g)
¼ teaspoon salt
1 teaspoon bread soda
1 teaspoon ginger
1 teaspoon cinnamon

Combine and beat the egg, sugar and treacle. In another bowl, combine and beat until melted the butter and hot water. Add to the egg mixture and beat until well blended. Sift the flour with the salt, soda and spices. Add in three parts to the first mixture, beating only until blended. Pour the batter into a lightly greased tin and bake for 50 minutes in a moderate oven (350°, gas mark 4).

For individual gingercakes, pour the batter into 12 greased muffin tins, filling them about two-thirds full. Bake for 15 minutes in a moderately hot oven (400°, gas mark 6).

A spicy, buttery fruit topping is a nice touch. To make the topping, combine and work with the hands until crumbly: 4

tablespoons of brown sugar, 1 teaspoon of cinnamon, 2 tablespoons of flour and 2 tablespoons of butter. Add 4 tablespoons
of chopped raisins. Spread the mixture over the gingerbread
10 minutes before it is cooked.

Ginger pound cake

6 oz flour (175g)
1 teaspoon ground ginger
1 teaspoon baking powder
4 oz butter or margarine (110g)
4 oz sugar (110g)
3 oz preserved ginger (75g)
2 oz washed and dried cherries (50g)
1 oz almonds (25g)
3 eggs
2 tablespoons milk (30 ml)

Sift the flour, ground ginger and baking powder. Cream the
butter and sugar, and add the preserved ginger cut small, the
quartered cherries and the blanched and sliced almonds. Beat
the eggs, mix in the milk and add, alternately with the flour to
the creamed mixture. Turn into a greased and lined tin and
bake for 1½ hours in a 375° oven (gas mark 5).

The top can be covered with water icing or royal icing and
decorated with cubes of preserved ginger and halved cherries.

Ginger sponge

4 oz butter or margarine (110g)
4 oz brown sugar (110g)
1 teaspoon golden syrup
1 egg
6 oz flour (175g)
½ teaspoon ground ginger
½ teaspoon bread soda
¼ pint sour milk (150 ml)

Cream the butter and sugar, and add the syrup and beaten
egg, mixing well. Sift the flour and the ground ginger. Blend
the bread soda with the milk, and add alternately with the
flour to the creamed mixture. Bake for one hour in a well-
greased tin in a 375° oven (gas mark 4).

Ginger/ walnut cake

1 lb flour (450g)
¼ teaspoon salt
½ teaspoon cinnamon
½ teaspoon allspice
1 teaspoon bread soda
4 oz butter or margarine (110g)
6 oz sugar (175g)
4 tablespoons treacle (60 ml)
6 tablespoons sour milk or buttermilk (90 ml)
2 eggs
1½ teaspoons ginger
2 tablespoons chopped preserved ginger
3 tablespoons chopped walnuts

Sift the flour, salt, spices and bread soda. Cream the butter and sugar. Stir the treacle into the sour milk. Mix with the beaten eggs and add alternately with the flour to the creamed mixture, beating very gently until smooth after each addition. Finally, mix in the ginger and the walnuts. Then turn into a shallow, well-greased tin, and bake for 25–30 minutes in a 350° oven (gas mark 4).

Old-fashioned gingerbread

12 oz flour (350g)
1 teaspoon cinnamon
1 teaspoon ginger
1 teaspoon bread soda
¼ teaspoon salt
4 oz sugar (110g)
2 eggs
6 tablespoons treacle (90 ml)
4 oz melted margarine or lard (110g)
½ pint buttermilk or sour milk (275 ml)

Sift the flour with the spices, bread soda and salt. Add the sugar. Mix together the eggs, treacle, melted shortening and buttermilk. Beat the whole lot together, turn into a greased tin and bake in a moderate oven (375°, gas mark 5).

Sunday	12 oz flour (350g)
gingerbread	1 teaspoon bread soda
	$\frac{1}{2}$ teaspoon salt
	1 teaspoon nutmeg
	$1\frac{1}{2}$ teaspoons ground ginger
	4 oz butter or margarine (110g)
	8 oz brown sugar (225g)
	1 teaspoon grated lemon rind
	2 eggs
	8 tablespoons treacle (120 ml)
	$\frac{1}{4}$ pint boiling water (150 ml)

Sift the flour, bread soda, salt and spices. Cream the butter, and add the sugar gradually, beating well. Beat in the grated lemon rind, and then the eggs, one at a time. Combine the treacle with the boiling water, and add alternately with the flour to the creamed mixture, beating well after each addition. Pour into a greased tin and bake for 45 minutes in a moderate oven (350°, gas mark 4).

Gingerbread men

There is no good reason why today's children should not enjoy what used to be the delight of the children of long ago.

Basic recipe	2 oz butter (50g)
	4 oz sugar (100g)
	4 tablespoons treacle (60 ml)
	1 lb flour (450g)
	1 teaspoon bread soda
	$\frac{1}{4}$ teaspoon ground cloves
	$\frac{1}{2}$ teaspoon cinnamon
	1 teaspoon ginger
	$\frac{1}{2}$ teaspoon salt
	5 tablespoons water (75 ml)

First, you must make a pattern from stiff paper or thin cardboard. Draw an outline 5 inches long of whatever figure you fancy — a little man, a clown, etc. Now fold the square in two so that the fold comes down the centre of the figure. With a sharp scissors, cut through the folded square. Unfold the pattern and you will find that it is perfectly symmetrical.

Cream together the butter and sugar, and beat in the treacle. Sift together the flour, bread soda, spices and salt. Add the flour to the creamed mixture in about 3 parts, alternately with the water. Chill the dough and roll it to about ¾ inch thick. Grease one side of the pattern and place it on the rolled dough. Cut around the outline with a sharp pointed knife, folding back the dough as you work. With a fish slice, transfer the cut-out figure to a greased baking sheet, and bake in a moderate oven (375° gas mark 4) for 8–10 minutes. Place on a rack to cool and dry before adding the trimmings.

For decoration, make some water icing by blending 4 table-spoons of icing sugar with just enough water to make a stiffish blend. With a toothpick or a small knife, add to the baked gingerbread men, caps, hair, moustaches, belts, shoes, etc. Better still, let the children add these touches!

Layer cakes

Banana sandwich

8 oz flour (450g)
½ teaspoon baking powder
¾ teaspoon bread soda
½ teaspoon salt
4 oz butter or margarine (110g)
6 oz castor sugar (175g)
2 eggs
1 cup mashed banana
1 teaspoon vanilla
2 tablespoons sour cream (30 ml)

Sift the flour with the baking powder, bread soda and salt. Cream the butter and sugar. Beat in the eggs, one at a time. Mix the bananas, vanilla and sour cream, and add alternately with the flour to the creamed mixture, beating until smooth after each addition. Bake in two 9 inch greased sandwich tins for 35 minutes in a 375° oven (gas mark 5). Fill with mashed banana to which castor sugar, a little lemon juice and rum (optional) has been added. Dust the top liberally with castor sugar.

Caramel layer cake

8 oz butter (225g)
6 oz sugar (175g)
4 eggs
10 oz flour (275g)
1½ teaspoons baking powder
3 tablespoons milk or cream (45 ml)
1 teaspoon vanilla

Cream the butter, gradually add the sugar, and beat until the mixture is light and fluffy. Add the beaten eggs and beat until smooth. Sift the flour and baking powder, and add in three parts to the creamed mixture alternately with the milk mixed with vanilla. Turn into 2 well-greased tins and bake for 1 hour in a 350° oven (gas mark 4).

When cold, put together with caramel filling (page 119) and cover the top with caramel icing (page 119).

Chocolate layer cake

4 oz butter or margarine (110g)
8 oz castor sugar (225g)
3 egg whites
1 teaspoon vanilla
12 oz flour (350g)
1 teaspoon baking powder
¼ teaspoon salt
⅔ cup milk (200 ml)
Walnuts

Cream the butter. Add the sugar slowly, beating in well. Add the unbeaten egg whites, one at a time, beating well after each addition. Add the vanilla. Sift together the flour, baking powder and salt, and add alternately with the milk to the creamed mixture. Cook in two well-greased 9 inch sandwich tins for 25 minutes in a moderate oven (375°, gas mark 4). When cool put together with chocolate filling (page 120). Cover the top and sides with icing (page 121) and decorate with halved walnuts.

Chocolate sandwich

4 oz butter (110g)
3 oz castor sugar (75g)
1 egg
6 oz flour (175g)
1 tablespoon cocoa (15 ml)
1 teaspoon baking powder
¼ teaspoon salt
3 tablespoons milk (45 ml)

Cream the butter and sugar and add the well-beaten egg. Sift together the flour, cocoa, baking powder and salt, and add alternately with the milk to the creamed mixture. Divide the mixture between 2 greased tins and bake for 20–25 minutes at 400° (gas mark 6). Put together with chocolate filling (page 120).

Cocoa sandwich

4 tablespoons cocoa (60 ml)
a little over ½ pint milk (280 ml)
4 oz butter or margarine (110g)
8 oz castor sugar (225g)
3 eggs

1 teaspoon vanilla
1 lb flour (450g)
$\frac{1}{4}$ teaspoon bread soda
1$\frac{1}{2}$ teaspoons baking powder

Blend the cocoa with $\frac{1}{4}$ pint of milk, and cook in a double saucepan until smooth and thick; let it cool. Cream the butter and add the sugar slowly, beating well. Add the unbeaten eggs, one by one, beating well after each addition. Add the flavouring. Sift the flour, bread soda and baking powder, and add alternately with the remainder of the milk. Add the cocoa mixture and mix well. Divide between 2 well-greased sandwich tins and bake for 25 minutes in a moderate oven (375°, gas mark 5). When cool, put together with sweetened whipped cream.

Lemon sandwich

Follow recipe for caramel layer cake (page 97), but decrease milk to 2 tablespoons. When all the ingredients are added, blend in 1 tablespoon of lemon juice. Put together with lemon filling (page 123) and cover with lemon icing (page 124). Decorate with slices of crystallized lemon.

Orange sandwich

Follow recipe for caramel layer cake (page 97), but substitute orange juice for milk, and add 1 tablespoon of grated orange rind. Put together with orange cream filling (page 124), and cover with orange icing (page 125).

Queen sandwich

4 oz butter or margarine (110g)
8 oz sugar (250g)
3 egg whites
1 teaspoon vanilla
1 lb flour (450g)
2 teaspoons baking powder
$\frac{1}{4}$ teaspoon salt
6 tablespoons milk (90 ml)

Cream the butter and add the sugar slowly, beating well. Add the unbeaten egg whites, one at a time, beating well after each addition. Add the vanilla. Sift the flour, baking powder and salt, and add alternately with the milk to the creamed mixture. Pour into two well-greased round sandwich tins and bake for 25 minutes in a moderate oven (about 375°, gas mark 5). When cool, put together with orange filling (page 125), and dust the top with castor sugar.

Silver sandwich

12 oz flour (350g)
1 teaspoon baking powder
½ teaspoon salt
6 oz butter or margarine (175g)
6 oz castor sugar (175g)
½ teaspoon almond essence
4 tablespoons milk (60 ml)
4 tablespoons water (60 ml)
6 egg whites

Sift the flour, baking powder and salt. Cream the butter until soft and smooth, and gradually add the sugar, beating until fluffy. Add the almond essence. Add the flour alternately with the combined milk and water, beating until smooth after each addition. Fold in thoroughly the stiffly-beaten egg whites. Turn into 3 paper-lined 8 inch sandwich tins, and bake for 30–35 minutes in a moderate oven (375°, gas mark 5). Put the layers together with lemon filling (page 123). Cover the top and sides with boiled icing (page 118).

Victoria sandwich

8 oz flour (225g)
1 teaspoon baking powder
¼ teaspoon salt
4 oz butter or margarine (110g)
8 oz castor sugar (225g)
1 teaspoon vanilla
2 eggs
3 tablespoons milk (45 ml)

Sift the flour, baking powder and salt. Cream the butter until soft and smooth and gradually add the sugar, beating until fluffy. Beat in the vanilla. Separate the eggs. Add the beaten yolks to the creamed mixture. Add the flour alternately with the milk, beating until smooth after each addition. Beat the egg whites until stiff and fold gently into the mixture. Cook in two greased 8 inch tins for about 30 minutes in a 375° oven (gas mark 5). When cold, put the layers together with raspberry jam and dust the top with castor or icing sugar.

Meringues

The basic rules for successful meringue making are:

(1) Use fine castor sugar.

(2) For a professional crispness, use 1 part icing sugar to 3 parts castor sugar.

(3) Since the faintest trace of grease will spoil meringues, scald and rinse the bowl, mixing spoon and beater.

(4) Separate the whites from the yolks the night before, and leave the whites, uncovered, in a bowl. This helps the water in the whites to evaporate and makes for easier beating.

Basic meringue recipe

3 oz castor sugar (75g)
1 oz icing sugar (25g)
2 egg whites
Whipped cream

Mix the castor sugar and icing sugar. Beat the two egg whites to stiff dry peaks. Add half the sugar gradually, beating well after each addition. Fold in the remainder of the sugar all at once, very gently.

Pipe the mixture with a meringue tube on to a baking tin covered with kitchen paper, or on to a very slightly greased baking tin. Failing a meringue tube, shape the meringues with a tablespoon. Cook for 1 hour at 240° (gas mark ½). Hollow them by pressing them with an egg or the back of a spoon and put them back in a very cool oven to finish drying off. Put two together with sweetened whipped cream or crushed sweetened fruit, or any desired filling.

Keep bread and cake in different containers – cake draws the moisture from bread.

Pancakes

It is a pity that crêpes Suzette — pancakes at their most gorgeous — should have such snobbish associations. If only they weren't so exclusively a restaurant dish! But there it is. Think of crêpes Suzette, and what do you see?

A select restaurant ... hovering waiters ... an obsequious maître d'hôtel whose coat, from habit, must surely bend over of itself when he takes it off at night. He stands with priestly reverence over a table bearing a chafing-dish where the final sacred rites in the making of crêpes Suzette are about to be celebrated.

The table is drawn close to a party of diners on whose behalf all this pomp and glory is being enacted. They have worked right through the menu. They have swum clear through the wine list. Now, from faces that are flushed and heavy with gastronomic exertion, their filmed eyes watch the maître d'hôtel prepare this crowning tribute to their greed and pockets.

He shoots back his cuffs, lifts spoon and fork and gently immerses the rolled pancakes in the silver cauldron of bubbling orange sauce.

As tenderly as a mother bathes her baby, he spoons the golden sauce over the pancakes until each is as saturated as he for whom it is intended would wish to be.

Now comes the big moment.

A black-coated acolyte approaches from each side. One bears a bottle of Cointreau. The other a bottle of brandy. Under a starched dicky, the heart of each beats wildly with the hope that one day he, too, may know the glory of officiating at such a chafing-dish . . . of preparing crêpes Suzette for just such a party of nice ladies and gentlemen.

The high-priest accepts the bottles, and allows a beautifully-judged trickle to descend from each into the dish.

A hush falls on the restaurant as he accepts from his third acolyte a box of matches. He lights one and touches it to the spirit-topped sauce. The sauce leaps into blue flame. He spoons the flames over the pancakes.

Quickly ... the hot plates!

Fearlessly, he lifts the crêpes, each dripping gouts of flaming syrup, transfers them to the serving dishes and places them before the gods who order them.

For a minute or two he hovers anxiously while the crêpes are tasted and ruminated on.

'Are the crêpes to your liking, sir?'

'Not a bad effort at all — rather wizard, in fact. Say, you chaps, how about another drink before we push along?'

'Rather an idea, that, old boy. Where's that bally waiter? Marjorie, old girl, did I ever tell you about the wizard show our chaps put up over in ..."

And now let us visit the pancake in its American setting.

Way out West, where men are men, and women know how to cook, a lone cowboy leaps from his wild mustang and announces his coming in a manly baritone which sends rocks rolling down the canyon and makes the timid coyote run yelping into the cactus.

A gingham-gowned girl comes running to greet him. 'Hi-ya, baby,' he yells. 'What's cookin'?'

'Apple flapjacks, honey,' she answers. 'Come and get them.'

'You're darn well tootin',' is the glad reply. 'Baby, here I come.'

American apple pancake	
	1 pint milk (570 ml)
	2 cups stale breadcrumbs
	1½ oz castor sugar (40g)
	2 tablespoons melted butter (30 ml)
	2 eggs
	4 oz flour (110g)
	½ teaspoon cinnamon
	2 teaspoons baking powder
	½ teaspoon salt
	2 cooking apples
	Honey or syrup

Bring the milk to boiling point, add the breadcrumbs and rub to a paste with a wooden spoon. Beat in the sugar and melted butter. Separate the eggs and beat the yolks until thick and lemon coloured before adding to the batter. Next add the flour sifted with the cinnamon and baking powder. Peel, core and chop the apples finely (better still, grate them); there should be about 1½ cups. Add to the batter. Beat the egg whites until stiff with the salt, and fold in gently. Drop in tablespoons on a slightly greased pan and cook until brown on both sides. Serve with honey or syrup; or butter and sprinkle with castor sugar.

Basic pancake recipe

6 oz flour (175g)
2 eggs
½ pint milk (275g)
Castor sugar
Lemon

Put the flour into a large jug. Break the eggs into the flour and stir well with a wooden spoon until the mixture is a smooth paste. Add the milk gradually, beating well. Cover the batter and leave in a cool place for at least one hour.

Grease a pan lightly with butter and place over a moderate heat until smoking hot. Pour in about two tablespoons of batter. Tilt the pan so that the batter completely covers the bottom of the pan. Cook over a moderate heat, shaking the pan occasionally. After about 1½ minutes, the underside should be cooked, so the pancake can be tossed or turned. Turn the pancake out on to paper sprinkled liberally with castor sugar. Roll quickly, keep warm in a covered dish and serve with sugar and wedges of lemon.

Boxty

In the North, they have immortalised boxty in a song which goes back to the days of Bonnie Prince Charlie:

> *I'll have none of your boxty,*
> *I'll have none of your blarney,*
> *But I'll throw my petticoats over my head*
> *And be off with my royal Charlie.*

Up there, boxty sometimes takes the place of the barmbrack as a prognosticator of the year's weddings. The girls are warned,

> *Boxty on the griddle, boxty on the pan,*
> *If you don't eat boxty, you'll never get your man.*

Boxty pancakes

4 oz grated raw potato (110g)
4 oz flour (110g)
1 teaspoon baking powder
1 teaspoon salt
4 oz mashed cooked potato (110g)
2 eggs
Milk to mix

Squeeze the grated raw potato in a cloth to remove as much moisture as possible. Sieve the flour with the baking powder and salt. Mix all the ingredients well together and add well-beaten eggs and sufficient milk to make a dropping batter. Drop by tablespoonfuls on a greased hot frying pan and cook over a moderate heat, allowing about 4 minutes each side. Serve hot and well buttered, with or without castor sugar.

Crêpes Suzette (simplified)

4 oz flour (110g)
½ teaspoon salt
1½ oz castor sugar (40g)
2 eggs
½ pint milk (275 ml)
2 tablespoons melted butter (30 ml)
½ teaspoon grated lemon rind
Wine glass of brandy or Cointreau

Sift together the flour, salt and 2 tablespoons of the sugar. Add the well-beaten eggs to the milk, and beat this into the flour mixture, using an egg-beater. Now add the melted butter and the grated lemon rind. Grease a heavy pan with butter. When the pan is very hot, cover the bottom with a thin layer of batter, tilting the pan so that the batter covers the pan evenly. Cook until golden brown on one side, then turn and cook on the other. Fold in quarters and keep hot in the oven or on a plate over boiling water. When serving, sprinkle with the remainder of the sugar, pour brandy or Contreau over them, ignite and serve at once.

Orange pancakes

Prepare pancakes as in crêpes Suzette recipe. When cooked, roll in neat cylinders. Serve with hot orange sauce (page 126).

German pancakes	3 eggs
	1 teaspoon salt
	1 dessertspoon sugar
	1½ pints milk (845 ml)
	1 lb flour (450g)
	1 tablespoon melted butter (15 ml)
	3 breakfast cups grated raw potato

Separate the eggs. To the well-beaten yolks, add the salt, sugar and milk. Gradually add the flour and melted butter, beating well. Stir in the grated potatoes. Fold in the egg whites which have been stiffly beaten. Bake at once on a hot greased griddle or heavy pan, allowing 3 minutes on each side. Serve hot and well buttered.

It is Shrove Tuesday, and the men from the fields tread quickly coming in, because they know there will be pancakes for supper — real pancakes, none of your paper-thin rolled foolishness, but good substantial buttermilk pancakes.

There's a clatter of them as high as your hip waiting on the hob, with melted butter and sugar trickling down the sides.

What matter if the women of the house have developed thawlock from beating and mixing and turning pancakes for the past two hours? It's all in a good cause.

Isn't it Pancake Night?

Irish pancakes	1 lb flour (450g)
	1 teaspoon salt
	1 teaspoon bread soda
	2 eggs
	Buttermilk to mix

Sift the flour with the salt and bread soda. Break the eggs into a well in the centre of the flour and mix well. Beat in enough buttermilk to make a thick batter. Fry in spoonfuls on a greased pan. Butter them as they come from the pan and sprinkle thickly with sugar.

Small cakes

One kind of cake for tea is nice. Six kinds are nicer. To impress a guest or delight a child with a variety of cakes does not call for great culinary skill. All you need is a batch of plain cup cakes. The variety is achieved by ringing the changes on the decorations.

Serve some with a topping of icing sugar sieved through a coffee strainer. Coat others with water icing and decorate with a few raisins or a halved cherry. For coffee cakes, mix the icing with strong coffee instead of with water. That plain icing can be the basis of a score of decorative tricks. While it is still wet sprinkle it with (a) hundreds-and-thousands, (b) shredded coconut, (c) chocolate curls and flakes made as follows: Break up a bar of plain chocolate and place it in a cup. Stand the cup in hot water until the chocolate melts. Pour it on the bottom of an inverted baking tin and spread it very thinly with a palette knife. As soon as the chocolate is hard, slice off curls and flakes as thinly as possible with a sharp knife.

Filled cup cakes are very effective. Take a thin slice from the top of the cooked cake and make a slight hollow. Fill the hollow with jam, lemon curd or sweetened whipped cream. Replace the top and sift icing sugar over it.

For a final touch of variety, give a few of the cakes a 'swirled' topping. This is much more effective than icing put on with a palette knife or spoon. Just dip the top of the cake in icing and give it a quick swirl.

There are as many basic mixtures as there are decorations. Here is a mixture which makes a soft even textured cake. Makes about 36 little cakes.

Basic mixture

9 oz castor sugar (250g)
5 oz butter or margarine (150g)
2 eggs
1 teaspoon vanilla
7 oz flour (200g)
2½ oz cornflour (65g)
1 teaspoon baking powder
4 tablespoons milk (60 ml)

Warm the sugar in the mixing bowl, then beat with the butter. Beat the eggs, mix in the vanilla and add a little at a time, beating them thoroughly but lightly into the creamed mixture. Sieve the flour, cornflour and baking powder, and lightly fold into the mixture, little by little, alternately with the milk.

Bake the cakes in muffin or patty tins, filled about two-thirds full. Or bake them in paper cases filled about half full. Give them from 18–20 minutes in a moderately hot oven (375°, gas mark 5). Prepare the tins by brushing them with melted butter (I strongly recommend butter instead of margarine for greasing the tins as the cooked cakes will have a much better appearance and flavour.) Dust the greased tins with flour until they are well coated, and then shake out the excess. For professional shape and symmetry, use a forcing bag or a large meringue tube to force the mixture into the tins or paper cases.

When the cakes are cooked, let them stand for a minute or two in the tins. Then take a sharp knife and loosen any that may need loosening. Turn them out carefully and let them cool on a wire tray before decorating. For a very quick and easy decoration, place a small piece of chocolate on a hot cake. As the chocolate melts, spread it with a palette knife. A halved almond or a crystallized violet placed in the centre will add the final touch.

Applesauce cakes

4 oz brown sugar (110g)
4 oz butter (110g)
1 egg
8 oz flour (225g)

½ teaspoon salt
1 teaspoon baking powder
1 teaspoon cinnamon
½ teaspoon ground cloves
4 oz raisins (110g)
2 oz currants (50g)
1 teacup of sieved stewed apple

Cream the sugar and butter and beat in the egg. Sift the flour, salt, baking powder and spices, and add to the creamed mixture. Mix in the fruit. Heat the stewed apple slightly and beat into the mixture. Bake in greased patty tins for 20 minutes in a 375° oven (gas mark 5).

Buttermilk teacakes

1 lb flour (450g)
½ teaspoon salt
1 teaspoon bread soda
½ teaspoon cream of tartar
3 oz butter or margarine (75g)
3 oz currants (75g)
4 oz sultanas (110g)
2 oz chopped peel (50g)
2 oz castor sugar (50g)
Buttermilk to make a stiff dough

Sift the flour, salt, bread soda and cream of tartar. Cream the butter, blend it with the flour, then add the currants, sultanas and chopped peel. Add the sugar. Mix to a stiff dough with buttermilk, knead lightly, roll out ½ inch thick and cut in rounds. Bake for 20 minutes in a 425° oven (gas mark 7). Serve hot, split and buttered.

Cherry cakes

2 oz washed and dried cherries (50g)
4 oz flour (110g)
1 teaspoon baking powder
3 oz butter or margarine (110g)
3 oz castor sugar (75g)
2 oz citron peel (50g)
1 egg
1 tablespoon milk (15 ml)

Wash the cherries and dry them to prevent them sinking to the bottom of the mixture. Sift the flour and baking powder. Cream the butter and sugar until soft and fluffy. Quarter the cherries and slice the peel finely. Add the beaten egg to the creamed mixture. Stir in the flour, fruit and milk. Fill patty tins two-thirds with the mixture and bake for 15 minutes in a hot oven (450°, gas mark 7).

To vary flavour, omit the peel and substitute 2 oz chopped crystallized ginger.

Chocolate cakes

2 oz plain chocolate (50g)
1 tablespoon milk (15 ml)
5 oz flour (150g)
1 teaspoon baking powder
4 oz butter or margarine (110g)
3 oz castor sugar (75g)
2 eggs
½ teaspoon vanilla

Melt the chocolate in the milk and let it cool. Sift the flour and baking powder. Beat the butter and sugar to a soft cream. Beat the eggs, mix in the vanilla, and add alternately with the flour to the creamed mixture, beating well. Now add the chocolate and milk, and mix until the batter is smooth and evenly-coloured. Fill greased patty tins or cases two-thirds full,and bake for 15–20 minutes in a 425° oven (gas mark 7). Ice with chocolate glacé icing (page 121).

Coconut tops

4 oz butter or margarine (110g)
3 oz castor sugar (75g)
2 eggs
5 oz flour (150g)
1 teaspoon baking powder
2 oz dessicated coconut (50g)
1 tablespoon milk (15 ml)

Cream the butter and sugar until light. Add the beaten eggs and beat until smooth. Mix in the flour which has been sifted with the baking powder. Lastly, stir in the coconut and milk.

Fill patty tins two-thirds full with the mixture and bake for 15 minutes in a 425° oven (gas mark 7). Ice with coconut icing (page 122).

Honey buns

8 oz flour (225g)
8 oz wheaten meal (225g)
3 teaspoons baking powder
¾ teaspoon salt
3 oz butter (75g)
¼ pint milk (150 ml)
1 egg

Sift the dry ingredients and rub in the butter. Add the milk and beaten egg, stirring quickly until the dough is soft but not sticky. Turn on to a floured board and knead gently. Roll out ¼ inch thick and cut in small rounds with a pastry cutter. Spread half with honey filling, made by creaming butter and beating into it an equal amount of honey. Cover with the remaining rounds and press the edges together with a fork. Place on a lightly greased baking sheet and bake for 20 minutes in a hot oven (450°, gas mark 8).

Variety may be given to the honey and butter mixture by the addition of any or all of the following: Lemon juice chopped nuts, chopped raisins, chopped dates.

Lemon cakes

4 oz flour (110g)
1 dessertspoon cornflour
1 teaspoon baking powder
⅛ teaspoon salt
2 oz butter or margarine (50g)
2 oz sugar (50g)
1 egg
2 tablespoons milk (30 ml)
Grated rind of ½ lemon

Sift the flour, cornflour, baking powder and salt. Cream the butter and sugar. Beat the egg with the milk, mix in the grated lemon rind, and add alternately with the flour to the creamed mixture. Bake in greased patty tins for 20 minutes in a 400° oven (gas mark 6). Top with lemon icing (page 124).

Raspberry nuggets

1 egg
2 oz butter or margarine (50g)
2 oz castor sugar (50g)
1 oz ground rice (25g)
4 oz flour (110g)
1 teaspoon baking powder
1 oz citron peel (25g)
2 tablespoons milk (30 ml)
3 tablespoons raspberry jam

Separate the egg and beat yolk and white separately. Cream the butter and sugar, stir in the egg yolk and beat well. Mix the rice, flour and baking powder and stir into the egg mixture. Add the shredded peel and milk and mix well. Finally, fold in the stiffly beaten egg white. Put a spoonful of the mixture in well-greased patty tins, add a dab of raspberry jam, and cover with another spoonful of mixture (only fill the tins two-thirds full). Bake for 15 minutes in a hot oven (400°, gas mark 6).

Sour milk spice cakes

4 oz butter or margarine (110g)
4 oz brown sugar (110g)
8 oz flour (225g)
½ teaspoon cinnamon
¼ teaspoon cloves
⅛ teaspoon salt
2 teaspoons baking power
½ teaspoon bread soda
2 eggs
1 teaspoon vanilla
4 tablespoons sour milk (60 ml)
4 oz currants (110g)

Cream the butter and sugar. Sift the flour, spices, salt, baking powder and bread soda. Beat the eggs, one at a time, into the creamed mixture, and stir in the vanilla. Add the flour in 3 lots alternately with the milk. Fold in the cleaned currants. Bake in greased patty tins for 20 minutes in a 375° oven (gas mark 5). Top with coffee icing (page 122) and decorate with a halved blanched almond or a piece of preserved ginger.

Sponge cakes

Sponge cake depends for its lightness on the amount of air incorporated during mixing, so to get in the maximum amount of air get the whisk down to the bottom of the bowl and lift it right up with each beat. Another essential is that the dry ingredients be well sifted. When the cake shrinks from the side of the tin it is done.

The perfect sponge cake is free from these main blemishes:

(1) A moist, sticky crust: This is usually caused by using more sugar than is called for in the recipe, or by using very coarse sugar.

(2) White spots on the crust: Coarse-grained sugar will cause these.

(3) Tough texture: This may be prevented by sifting in the flour lightly, by beating the eggs to the right degree of thickness and by baking at the correct temperature.

(4) Coarse, uneven texture: This may be due to any one of three faults; too little mixing, the use of too much baking powder, too slow an oven.

(5) A tough, unrisen cake: Too hot an oven is the chief cause.

Basic sponge recipe	4 eggs 4 oz castor sugar (110g) 3 oz flour (75g)

Put the eggs and sugar in a bowl and beat over hot water for 20 minutes or until really stiff and light-coloured. Fold in the flour. For a soft crust, turn into a floured ungreased tin. For the typical sponge crust, butter the tin, then coat it with 1 dessertspoon of flour mixed with 1 dessertspoon of castor sugar. Bake for 45 minutes at 375° (gas mark 5).

Chocolate sponge
Follow the basic sponge recipe, substituting 1 oz (25g) of cocoa for 1 oz of flour. Sift the cocoa and the flour together at least three times.

Feathery spoonge

8 oz flour (225g)
1 teaspoon baking powder
$\frac{1}{4}$ teaspoon salt
3 eggs
8 oz castor sugar (225g)
2 teaspoons lemon juice
6 tablespoons hot milk (90 ml)

Sift together three times, the flour, baking powder and salt. Beat the eggs until very thick and light. Add the sugar gradually, beating constantly, and then the lemon juice. Fold in the flour, a little at a time. Add the hot milk and stir quickly until thoroughly blended. Pour into an ungreased tin and bake for 35 minutes in a moderate oven (350°, gas mark 4). Remove from the oven and invert the pan with its edges resting on milk bottles, so that the cake hangs free of the table. When quite cold, loosen the sides of the cake with a spatula and turn out.

Hot milk sponge cake

2 eggs
6 oz castor sugar (175g)
6 tablespoons hot milk (90 ml)
$\frac{1}{4}$ teaspoon lemon extract
$\frac{1}{2}$ teaspoon vanilla extract
6 oz flour (175g)
1 teaspoon baking powder
$\frac{1}{4}$ teaspoon salt

Separate the eggs and beat the yolks thoroughly. Add the sugar to the yolks alternately with the hot milk, and beat until thick and lemon-coloured. Add the lemon and vanilla flavourings. Sift the flour, baking powder and salt, and mix gently with the egg mixture. Finally, fold in the stiffly-beaten egg whites. Bake in a shallow buttered tin for about 30 minutes in a moderate oven (325°, gas mark 3).

Hot water sponge cake

5 eggs
$\frac{1}{4}$ teaspoon salt
$\frac{1}{4}$ teaspoon cream of tartar
6 oz castor sugar (175g)
2 tablespoons hot water (30 ml)

1½ teaspoons grated lemon rind
1 tablespoon lemon juice (15 ml)
4 oz flour (110g)

Separate the eggs. Put the whites into a large bowl, sprinkle with the salt and beat until foamy. Add the cream of tartar and beat until stiff enough to form peaks. Continue beating, adding half of the sugar, a tablespoon at a time, until it is just blended. Beat the egg yolks until thick and light with the remainder of the sugar, the hot water and lemon rind. Beat in the lemon juice. Add the sifted flour to the egg yolks, and when it is well-blended, fold it gently into the egg whites. Bake in an ungreased tin for 1 hour in a slow oven (325°, gas mark 3). When baked, invert the tin over a rack until cold.

One egg
sponge cake

---

5 oz flour (150g)
1 teaspoon cream of tartar
1 egg
⅛ teaspoon salt
4 oz castor sugar (110g)
1 teaspoon bread soda
¼ pint sour milk (150 ml)
1 tablespoon melted butter (15 ml)

Sift the flour and cream of tartar. Break the egg into a basin, add the salt and the sugar and beat well for 5 minutes. Dissolve the bread soda in the milk and add it to the egg. Now stir in the flour and add the melted butter when thoroughly blended. Turn into two sandwich tins which have been greased with melted butter and sprinkled with equal amounts of castor sugar and flour. Bake for 15 minutes in a hot oven (400°, gas mark 6). Put together with jam and sprinkle the top with icing sugar.

Orange cream sponge ball

Follow basic sponge recipe. Turn gently into a greased and floured Swiss roll tin and bake for 15 minutes in a 450° oven (gas mark 8). When cooked, turn on to a cloth dredged with sugar, snip off the edges, spread with orange cream filling (page 124) and roll up quickly.

Swiss roll

Follow basic sponge recipe. Turn into a Swiss roll tin and bake for 15 minutes in a hot oven (450°, gas mark 8). When cooked, turn on to a cloth or paper dredged with castor sugar. Snip off the edges, spread with raspberry jam and roll up quickly.

Treacle sponge roll

4 eggs
4 tablespoons treacle (60 ml)
1 teaspoon lemon juice
1 oz sugar (25g)
6 oz flour (175g)
½ teaspoon salt
½ teaspoon bread soda
¼ teaspoon cinnamon
¼ teaspoon nutmeg
¼ teaspoon ground cloves
½ pint cream (275 ml)
1 oz preserved ginger

Separate the eggs. Beat the yolks until light, then add the treacle and beat thoroughly. Beat the egg whites until stiff, and gradually add the lemon juice and the sugar. Fold the egg yolks into the whites. Sift the flour, salt, bread soda and spices, and fold into the egg mixture. Turn into a shallow greased tin lined with greased paper. Bake for 25–30 minutes in a slow oven (325°, gas mark 3).

Turn out on to a towel dusted with powdered sugar, roll up and leave to cool. Whip the cream until thick and mix with it the chopped preserved ginger. Carefully unroll the treacle roll, spread with the cream mixture and roll again. Dust with cinnamon and castor sugar.

Wine sponge

6 eggs (separated)
4 oz castor sugar (110g)
½ glass port wine
4 oz sifted flour (110g)
¼ teaspoon salt
½ teaspoon cinnamon

Beat the egg yolks until thick. Add the sugar and beat well, then the wine, flour, salt and cinnamon. Beat the egg whites until stiff but not dry, and fold into the yolk mixture. Turn into an ungreased 10 inch tube tin and bake for 1 hour at 350° (gas mark 3). Invert pan until cake is cold.

Fillings and icings

Almond icing *(marizpan)*	1 lb icing sugar (450g) 1½ lb ground almonds (675g) 8 oz castor sugar (225g) 4 eggs 1 teaspoon vanilla 1 dessertspoon rum 1 dessertspoon orange-flower water Juice of 1 lemon

Crush the icing sugar with a rolling pin and sieve well. Mix the almonds and castor sugar. Beat the eggs and add gradually, with the flavourings. Mix to a paste, first with a wooden spoon, then with the hand. Having kneaded the paste, wrap in greaseproof paper, put into a covered jar or tin and leave until next day when it will be easier to handle.

A word of warning: While it is essential to work the marzipan into a smooth paste, it must not be overhandled. Otherwise it will become crumbly and brittle.

Icing a Christmas cake

The cake needs a little special preparation before putting on the almond icing. For best results, you need an even surface. If the cake has not risen evenly, you can either turn it upside down, or camouflage any unevenness with the icing. If, in spite of precautions, there are any burnt spots, grate them off with a fine bread-grater. Brush off any loose crumbs, and then give the cake a coat of slightly beaten egg white or warm jelly or warm sieved jam — this makes the icing stick.

Knead the icing a little, divide into two, and on a pastry board sprinkled with castor sugar roll out one piece into a round large enough to cover the top of the cake. Put it on the cake and run a rolling pin lightly over it to make it even. Now take a piece of string and measure the circumference of your cake. Roll out the icing for the sides in two even pieces — these will be easier manage than one long strip. Press the two lengths of icing into position and make the sides smooth and symmetrical by rolling a jam jar or milk bottle around them. The cake may now be covered and put away in a dry place for a week or so. It is then ready for royal icing (page 126).

Almond paste filling (substitute)

2 oz butter or margarine (50g)
2 oz semolina (50g)
8 tablespoons stale breadcrumbs
2 oz castor sugar (50g)
4 tablespoons water (60 ml)
1½ teaspoons almond essence
½ teaspoon vanilla

Mix the ingredients and bring slowly to the boil, stirring constantly until the mixture forms a ball of paste. A few drops of yellow colouring may be added.

Boiled icing

8 oz sugar (225g)
1 tablespoon golden syrup (15 ml)
4 tablespoons water (60 ml)
2 egg whites
¼ teaspoon cream of tartar
⅛ teaspoon salt
1 teaspoon vanilla

Put the sugar, syrup and water in a saucepan and stir over a low heat until the sugar is dissolved. Boil, covered, for about 3 minutes, then boil, uncovered and without stirring, until the syrup reaches soft ball stage (238°), or when a small amount of syrup dropped into cold water forms a soft ball when pressed between fingers and thumb. Remove from the heat.

Quickly beat the egg whites with the cream of tartar until stiff but not dry, and then pour the syrup over them in a fine stream, beating constantly. Add the salt and vanilla and continue beating until the frosting is cool and of the right consistency to spread. If it hardens before spreading, beat in a few drops of hot water. For a good effect, heap the frosting around the edge of the top of the cake; then swirl it over top and sides with the back of a spoon.

Butter cream

4 oz butter (110g)
3 oz icing sugar (75g)

Cream the butter and the sieved icing sugar until light and creamy. Flavour and colour to taste.

Caramel filling (1)

4 oz brown sugar (110g)
5 tablespoons cream (75 ml)
2 teaspoons butter
1/8 teaspoon salt
1/2 teaspoon vanilla

Combine and stir together the sugar, cream, butter and salt, and cook slowly to boiling point. Cool slightly and add the vanilla. Beat to spreading consistency.

Caramel filling (2)

6 oz butter or margarine (175g)
12 oz icing sugar (350g)
Hot water
1 teaspoon vanilla

Melt and stir the butter until golden brown. Sift the sugar and blend in. Remove from heat and add, 1 tablespoon at a time, sufficient hot water to make a filling of spreading consistency. Add the vanilla.

Caramel icing (clear)

4 oz sugar (110g)
2 tablespoons water (30 ml)

Cook the sugar and water in a heavy saucepan over a moderate heat until it is clear and brown but not burnt. This icing is brittle and must be spread with a spatula while hot.

Chocolate butter icing

4 oz butter (110g)
6 oz icing sugar (225g)
2 oz chocolate (50g)
1 tablespoon hot water (15 ml)
1/2 teaspoon vanilla

Beat the butter to a very soft cream, and gradually beat in the sieved icing sugar. Break up the chocolate, dissolve it in hot water, and beat until smooth. When cold, add it and the vanilla to the icing, beating until evenly mixed and coloured.

Chocolate filling (1)

3 oz grated chocolate (75g)
1½ tablespoons water (25 ml)
5 oz icing sugar (150g)
3 oz butter or margarine (75g)

Mix the grated chocolate with the water and warm gently over a low heat until it darkens. Remove from the heat, beat in the sifted icing sugar and leave until cool. Cream the butter, add the chocolate mixture and beat until light and creamy.

Chocolate filling (2)

3 oz flour (75g)
3 oz drinking chocolate (75g)
4 oz sugar (110g)
½ teaspoon salt
1 pint scalded milk (570 ml)
2 egg yolks
1 teaspoon vanilla

Mix the flour, chocolate, sugar and salt, and blend to a paste with some of the milk. Add the paste to the rest of the milk and cook until thick in the top of a double saucepan, stirring constantly. Beat the egg yolks, add a little of the cooked mixture to them, then put everything into the saucepan. Cook for a further 3 minutes, stirring well. Add the vanilla, and cool.

Chocolate fudge icing

1 lb sugar (450g)
4 oz grated chocolate (110g)
4 tablespoons golden syrup (60 ml)
6 tablespoons milk (90 ml)
1 oz butter (25g)
1 teaspoon vanilla

Mix the sugar, chocolate, golden syrup and milk, add the butter and stir until the sugar is dissolved. Cook over a low heat until the mixture reaches soft ball stage (238°). Remove from the heat and cool. When cold, add the vanilla and beat until creamy and of good spreading consistency. If the icing hardens too quickly, add a few drops of hot water or stand the saucepan in hot water.

Chocolate glacé icing.	**4 oz grated chocolate (110g)** **4 oz icing sugar (110g)** **¼ teaspoon vanilla** **Cold water**

Melt the chocolate over hot water, beating with a wooden spoon. Stir in the sieved sugar, the vanilla and enough cold water to make the icing the consistency of thin cream. Use while lukewarm.

Chocolate icing	**4 oz grated chocolate (110g)** **2 tablespoons water (30 ml)** **4 oz icing sugar (110g)**

Mix together the grated chocolate and water. Stir the paste gently over a low heat until it becomes dark and runny, but do not let it get hot or the icing will be dull. Gradually beat in the sieved icing sugar and beat until the mixture is of a smooth spreading consistency. Use while still warm.

Chocolate icing (quick)	**5 oz grated chocolate (150g)** **2½ tablespoons water (37 ml)** **5 oz icing sugar (150g)**

Mix the chocolate with the water and warm gently over a low heat until dark and runny. Do not overheat. Beat in the sifted sugar and continue to beat until the mixture is of good spreading consistency.

Christmas log filling	**1 egg white** **6 tablespoons cream (90 ml)** **¼ oz gelatine (7g)** **2 teaspoons milk** **½ teaspoon vanilla** **6 oz castor sugar (175g)** **1 teaspoon rum**

Whip the egg white stiffly, and combine gently with the whipped cream. Soak the gelatine in barely enough water to cover it, then dissolve it in 2 teaspoons of lukewarm milk. When cool, add it with the vanilla, sugar and rum to the egg-cream mixture.

Coconut icing

8 oz icing sugar
1 tablespoon cream (15 ml)
2 oz shredded coconut (50g)
1 egg white

Sieve the sugar. Add the cream and coconut and enough stiffly beaten egg white to form a soft but not sticky paste.

Coconut icing (fluffy)

8 oz icing sugar (225g)
¼ pint water (150 ml)
2 oz shredded coconut (50g)
1 egg white

Sieve the icing sugar. Combine with the water and stir over a low heat until the sugar is melted. Bring to the boil and boil for 4 minutes without stirring. Remove from the heat and beat until the icing is thick and white. Stir in the coconut, and lastly fold in the stiffly beaten egg white.

Coffee filling

Follow the recipe for custard filling (page 123), substituting ¼ pint (150 ml) of strong coffee for the ¼ pint of milk.

Coffee icing

3 oz butter or margarine (75g)
8 oz icing sugar (225g)
⅛ teaspoon salt
3 tablespoons strong coffee (45 ml)
1 teaspoon vanilla or rum

Beat the butter until soft. Gradually add the sifted icing sugar, then the salt and coffee. Beat for 2 minutes, then add the vanilla or rum. Let it stand for 5 minutes, and beat again before spreading.

Custard filling (confectioner's cream)

¾ **pint milk (425 ml)**
1¼ **tablespoons cornflour (30g)**
¼ **teaspoon salt**
4 **oz sugar (110g)**
2 **egg yolks**
½ **teaspoons vanilla**

Scald the milk. Combine and add the cornflour and sugar, and when they are well blended, pour over them the slightly beaten egg yolks. Stir and cook the custard in a double saucepan until thick. Cool and beat in vanilla.

Date filling

1 **lb dates (450g)**
1 **tablespoon lemon juice (15 ml)**
6 **oz brown sugar (175g)**
1 **oz butter (25g)**
½ **pint water (275 ml)**

Wash, stone and chop the dates. Add the lemon juice, sugar, butter and water. Simmer, stirring constantly, for 10 minutes or until the mixture forms a thick paste. Cool before using.

Lemon filling (1)

4 **egg yolks**
3 **oz castor sugar (75g)**
2 **tablespoons lemon juice (30 ml)**
1 **teaspoon grated lemon rind**

Beat the egg yolks until thick and lemon coloured. Gradually beat in the sugar. Blend in the lemon juice and rind. Cook over hot water, stirring constantly until thick (about 8 minutes). Cool before using.

Lemon filling (2)

6 **oz sugar (225g7**
2 **oz cornflour (50g)**
⅛ **teaspoon salt**
1 **egg**
4 **tablespoons water (60 ml)**
3 **tablespoons lemon juice (45 ml)**
1 **teaspoon grated lemon rind**
½ **oz butter (13g)**

Combine the sugar, cornflour and salt in the top of a double saucepan. Stir in the well-beaten egg, water and lemon juice. Cook over boiling water for 5 minutes, stirring constantly; then for a further 10 minutes, stirring occasionally, until the mixture is thick. Remove from the heat, and add the lemon rind and butter. Stir until the butter is dissolved.

If a creamier filling is desired, fold in ½ cup of whipped cream when filling is cold.

Lemon filling (3)

2 eggs
8 oz castor sugar (225g)
Juice of 2 lemons
2 oz butter (50g)

Beat the eggs, then add the sugar, lemon juice and butter. Place the bowl in a saucepan containing hot water, and stir over a low heat until the mixture is smooth and thick. Use when cold.

Lemon icing (1)

1½ lb icing sugar (675g)
Lemon juice

Sieve the sugar and add enough lemon juice to form a thick paste. Beat until smooth.

Lemon icing (2)

1 eg white
2 teaspoons lemon juice
8 oz icing sugar (225g)

Beat the egg white until frothy and sprinkle with the lemon juice. Gradually beat in the icing sugar and continue beating until mixture is smooth and thick.

Orange cream filling

4 oz castor sugar (110g)
2½ tablespoons cornflour
Pinch of salt
1 egg yolk
4 tablespoons orange juice (60 ml)
1 tablespoon lemon juice (15 ml)
¼ pint water (150 ml)
1 teaspoon grated orange rind
½ oz butter (13g)

Combine the flour and cornflour, and add the salt and slightly beaten egg. Add the orange and lemon juice and water. Cook over boiling water until thick (about 12 minutes) stirring constantly. Add the orange rind and butter. Cool before using.

Orange filling	3 oz castor sugar (75g) 3 oz flour (75g) ¼ teaspoon salt ½ pint scalded milk (275 ml) ½ pint orange juice (275 ml) 2 eggs

Put the sugar, flour and salt in the top of a double saucepan, and mix well. Blend in the milk and stir until smooth. Stir in the orange juice, and cook the mixture over boiling water for 10 minutes, stirring frequently. Beat the eggs; add a little of the hot mixture to them and mix well. Pour into the saucepan and cook for 2 minutes, stirring constantly.

Orange icing (1)	12 oz icing sugar (350g) 1 tablespoon melted butter (15 ml) 1 tablespoon grated orange rind 1 tablespoon orange juice (15 ml) 1 tablespoon lemon juice (15 ml)

Put the sifted icing sugar, melted butter, orange rind, orange and lemon juice in the top of a double saucepan. Beat over hot water for 10 minutes, then remove from the heat and beat until cool and of a good spreading consistency.

Orange icing (2)	16 oz icing sugar (450g) 1 tablespoon melted butter (15 ml) 1 tablespoon grated orange rind 4 tablespoons orange juice (60 ml)

Put the sieved icing sugar, melted butter, grated orange rind and orange juice into the top of a double saucepan. Stir over hot water for 10 minutes. Remove from heat and beat until the icing is creamy and of a good spreading consistency.

Orange sauce

4 oz butter or margarine (110g)
4 oz castor sugar (110g)
4 tablespoons orange juice (60 ml)
1 dessertspoon lemon juice
1 desertspoon grated orange rind.

Melt the butter over a slow heat. Add the castor sugar and stir until dissolved. Add the orange juice, lemon juice and orange rind. Bring to a boil, and pour over the pancakes.

Pineapple icing

4 oz butter or margarine (110g)
1 lb icing sugar (450g)
1 teaspoon lemon juice
⅛ teaspoon salt
½ teaspoon vanilla
6 tablespoon pineapple

Cream the butter, and gradually add the sieved icing sugar and beat until creamy. Beat in the lemon juice, salt, vanilla and the pineapple, which has been drained and chopped.

Royal icing

4 egg whites
2 lb icing sugar (900g)
¼ teaspoon acetic acid
3 drops laundry blue

Place the carefully separated egg whites in a basin, and beat slightly until liquid. Crush and sieve the icing sugar. Add half of the sugar and beat lightly for 2 minutes. Add the remainder of the sugar gradually, beating well after each addition. Before the icing is quite stiff enough, add the acetic acid. At the last minute (to make sure that the icing will be as white as the driven snow) beat in 3 drops of ordinary laundry blue. Do not worry if the icing looks a little too blue — this will disappear in beating and the icing will dry out quite white. But do not use more than 3 drops of rather weak blue or the icing may have a greyish tinge.

Tips for perfect royal icing.

(1) Do not use lemon juice — it tends to turn the icing yellow.

(2) Do not omit to scald thoroughly the bowl in which the icing is to be made. The slightest trace of grease will spoil the appearance of the icing.

(3) Do not let a speck of egg yolk into the whites — this would spoil that glossy, pure white finish.

(4) Do not skimp on the beating. Royal icing must be beaten until it becomes smooth and snowy and stiff.

(5) Do not use more than the minimum of sugar necessary to get the icing to the required consitency. It is the light and thorough beating which gives good icing, and not the addition of extra sugar.

This recipe gives a sufficient quantity of icing for a large Christmas cake.

To apply royal icing

Stand the cake on a revolving icing table or on an upturned plate placed on a solid inverted bowl. Since the icing, if it is the right consistency, must be so thick that it is liable to dry out, keep a well-wetted cloth over the basin while you are working. Use a palette knife for spreading the icing. Keep a jug of hot water at hand and dip the knife into this now and then, shaking well to remove any drops after each dipping.

If you are icing both the top and sides of the cake, put the greater part of the icing on the top. Spread it smoothly, then coat the sides, turning the cake around with your left hand as you work. To secure a nice smooth top, hold the palette knife so that the end of the blade is at the centre of the cake; then revolve the cake, pressing very lightly on the knife. Do not lift the palette knife off the cake as you finish; draw it lightly towards you to avoid leaving a line.

Most people are satisfied with one coat of icing, but you may, if you wish, add another coat after the first coat has been allowed to dry out for a day or two. A very smooth top may be obtained by adding a coat of icing that is almost, but not quite, thin enough to pour. Having put this on top of the cake, lift the plate and give it a few smart taps on the bowl; the icing should flow perfectly smooth.

For special piped decorations, the icing should be stiffer than for coating. Piping must not be attempted until the icing proper is quite dry. For a good effect, do your writing or trellis work with a no. 2 writing tube in white icing. Then, when this is dry, go over it with pink icing, using a no. 1 tube. Having selected your design, transfer it on to the cake by placing the design on top of the cake and pricking it out with a darning needle.

White icing

4 oz icing sugar (110g)
¼ teaspoon vanilla
Cold water

Sift the sugar, add the vanilla and enough cold water to give a spreading consistency.

Pastry

But for the love of cowslips which has ruled me all my life, I might never have become acquainted with Mrs. McKey's fruit roll. And Ballyderrig might never have made friends with the occupants of Grange.

Everyone was excited when the McKeys came from Dublin to live in Grange. The old house had stood empty for years. 'It will be a good thing to have city people living among us,' my mother said, ''Twill liven us up a bit. Dublin people are great for parties and entertaining.'

She could not have been more mistaken. The McKeys added little or nothing to Ballyderrig's social life. They drove into the village on a side-car hired at Kildare station, the father sitting on one side, the mother and grown-up daughter sitting on the other. There was a bleak look about the three of them that, as things turned out, did not lie.

Never once in the weeks that followed did they give a sign of wanting to have anything to do with us. When Mrs. McKey did her shopping, she walked hurriedly among us with no more than a quiet 'Good-day' — a fragile little women she was, with a harassed air. Mr. McKey was just as aloof on those rare occasions when he came into the place. He was heavy-footed, as if burdened, and his lined face had a grim shut-in look. The daughter was never seen at all. 'She must think herself too good to walk on the same street as country people,' was our comment.

Grange had always been a great place for cowslips. The big old chestnut trees which paraded the avenue held warmth in their roots, and the donkey-brown branches dripped moisture to soften the earth and coax up the cowslips long before they appeared anywhere else. While Grange had stood empty, we children had made our own of the cowslips, but the coming of the McKeys created difficulties.

'You keep far away from Grange,' my mother warned me. 'They'll only run you. The McKeys don't want us. And maybe we don't want them.'

For my birthday that year (I was born in May) I had been given a Red Riding Hood doll. Her lovely clothes could be taken off. Every garment down to the little lace-edged knickers had tapes and buttons. On the day after my birthday I took the doll down to Loughlin's to show her to my friend Mary Jo.

My way led past Grange. I looked in through the gate. What I saw sent my mother's warning out of my head. Every chestnut tree stood in a golden ring of cowslips. I pushed open the gate. Leaving my doll sleeping in a mossy cleft between the great roots, I bent to pick. The stems were as smooth and cool as I had known they would be, and every nod of the gentle fringed heads released the loveliest smell in the world.

And then I heard voices right beside me. I jumped and turned. Mrs. McKey and her daughter were standing there. The young woman had my Red Riding Hood doll in her arms. She was hugging it to her and resisting all her mother's attempts to take it from her.

'Come on, Annie,' the mother urged. Her face was the saddest I had ever seen. 'Give the little girl her doll. I'll get you another.'

My seven-year-old sense of importance was flattered that a grown-up should wish to play with my doll. How was I to have known that 20-year-old Annie's mind had stopped growing when she was five? 'She can play with it for a while,' I conceded.

Mrs. McKey hesitated. 'Come into the house, then,' she said. 'It's tea-time.' She gave us tea, a lovely tea. There was fruit roll, and an apple flan in which the apples were a lovely red colour. I learned afterwards that she managed this by cooking a few slices of beetroot with the apples. When the tea was over, Annie and Mr. McKey and I played tiddley-winks. I found that he was not grim at all — only quiet and kind.

When it was time for me to go home, Annie cried because I was taking away my doll, and I had to promise to come back the next day.

I told my mother about my afternoon. As she listened, her face grew almost as sad as Mrs. McKey's. 'May Heaven comfort them,' she said. 'So that's what's wrong!' She had a great kindness and a great understanding, my mother. That night she did not go to bed until all hours. When I went to Grange next day, I had a present for Annie from my mother — a doll dressed in even lovelier clothes than my Red Riding Hood.

That was the start of a great friendship between the McKey's and the people of Ballyderrig. Annie was never lonely again. There were always children who were glad to play at Grange — as much, I honestly believe, out of liking for Annie as out of appreciation of the lovely teas Mrs. McKey gave us. And when, a couple of years later, the 'flu epidemic took the overgrown child to Heaven, we were still made welcome at Grange. Mrs McKey cooked nothing that we liked better than the rich spicy fruit roll. Easy to make, it was too. Just an oblong of shortcrust pastry brushed with melted butter, and covered with a layer of chopped raisins, nuts, candied peel and apples, sweetened with a sprinkling of brown sugar and enlivened with a dusting of cinnamon. Wet the edges, roll up and bake for 45 minutes in a moderate oven.

Pastry

In this section I have given the recipies for the various types of pastry first. Individual flans, pies and tarts are then listed alphabetically.

Nearly every cook has her (or his) own favourite fat or mixture of fats for pastry. I have given a choice of either butter or margarine in the following recipes (and in some cases, lard), but this is purely a matter for individual taste. Some people like all butter, some all margarine, some a mixture of butter and margarine or butter and lard or margarine and lard. It is a personal choice.

Good cooks tell you they hate cooking to precise measurements. No wonder! A pie crust can be thick or the thinnest of the thin. Flans and pies can be stuffed to bursting point with fruit or filling or contain a mere elegant sufficiency. So don't take my quantities as gospel — follow your own preferences.

Cheese pastry	8 oz flour (225g) ⅛ teaspoon salt 6 ozs cream cheese (175g) 2 ozs butter or margarine (50g) 2 tablespoons cold water (30 ml)

Sift the flour with the salt, and cut in the cream cheese and the butter. Stir in the cold water and mix lightly to a stiff dough. Chill thoroughly. Use for savoury pies and cheese sticks.

Choux pastry

Only a psychiatrist could explain why it is that so many competent cooks regard certain recipes as beyond their powers. Eclairs and cream puffs are among the 'fancies' which are mistakenly supposed to belong exclusively in the repertoire of the professional confectioner.

The truth is that any schoolgirl could make these sweet scraps of airiness — always provided that said schoolgirl took care to:

(1) Have all ingredients at room temperature.

(2) Cook the batter to a stiff paste before attempting to form the éclairs or puffs.

(3) Use a forcing bag and tube so that the finished cakes will have that uniform symmetry which distinguishes the expert's slickness from the novice's clumsiness.

The partially pre-cooked paste which is used for éclairs and cream puffs is called choux pastry, and here is the recipe:

Choux recipe	4 oz butter or margrine (110g) ½ pint water (275 ml) 5 oz flour (150g) 3 eggs

Put the butter into a saucepan with the water and bring to the boil. Quickly stir in the sifted flour all at once. Cook and stir over a low heat until the mixture is smooth and elastic, and until it comes cleanly away from the sides of the pan. This shows that all the moisture has been driven out — which is the purpose of this pre-oven cooking. Cool, stir occasionally. Then beat in the eggs, one by one, taking care to beat one egg until it is well blended before adding the next.

Cream puffs

Pipe small rounds of the mixture on to a baking sheet,or form the cream puffs with a spoon. For real puffiness, the puffs should be cooked in their own steam. To achieve this, invert a large patty tin over each puff, and cover the whole lot with a large inverted roasting tin before putting in the oven. Bake for 20–25 minutes in a moderate oven at 375° (gas mark 5). When cold, slit and fill with whipped cream. Spread the tops with white icing (page 128), or caramel icing (page 119).

Éclairs

Pipe the mixture into 3 inch fingers on to a greased baking tin and bake for 20–25 minutes at 375° (gas mark 5). When cool, slit down the sides and fill with whipped cream, custard filling (page 123), coffee filling (page 122) or chocolate filling (page 120). Spread the tops with chocolate or coffee icing (page 121/122).

Danish pastry

At first glace, the time and trouble involved in the making of Danish pastry may not seem justified. But it will be found in practice that the process is really simple and that the actual making of the pastry does not take up very much time. Unlike other mixtures containing yeast, the 'proving' of this dough must be done at a cold temperature — it will take longer, therefore, for the pastry to raise — perhaps even as long as six hours. This is to ensure that the fat and flour will remain in separate layers and thus result in the delicate flakiness which is the special feature of this confection. But since you may always carry on with your other jobs while the pastry is proving, this is no real drawback.

Danish pastry

1 oz castor sugar (26g)
1 tablespoon dried yeast
½ pint lukewarm milk (275 ml)
2 eggs
1 lb flour (450g)
½ teaspoon salt
8 oz butter or margarine (225g)

Dissolve the sugar in ¼ pint of milk; whisk in the yeast and leave to froth. Beat the eggs and add to the remainder of the milk, keeping back about 1 teaspoon of beaten egg to use for brushing the top of the pastry.

Sieve the flour with the salt. Take ¾ of the flour and add the yeast mixture and the milk and eggs. Mix to a smooth soft dough, adding a little more tepid milk if necessry. Roll out this dough to a square ¼ inch thick.

Cream the butter with the remaining 4 oz of flour and pat the creamed mixture to a square about 3 inches smaller than the dough. Lay in the centre, and then fold in the edges of the dough, left and right, top and bottom, towards the centre, making a kind of neat parcel. Roll out thinly, and leave in a cool place (preferably the fridge) for about 20 minutes, then fold and roll again. Let the dough rest for another 20 minutes, then fold and roll for a third time. It can now be cut to shape or left to chill for a couple of hours.

Danish crescents
Roll the dough ⅛ inch thick and cut in 5 inch wide strips. Cut the strips into squares and cut each square into two to form triangles. The crescents may be filled with almond paste, apricot jam or mincement. Place a spoonful on the base of the triangle, roll up towards the tip and bend in the shape of a crescent. Place the crescents on a greased baking tin, brush with beaten egg and leave in a cold place until they have doubled their bulk. Cook for 15 minutes in a 475° oven (gas mark 9).

When you take the pastries from the oven, brush them with a syrup made by dissolving 1 tablespoon of sugar in 1 table-spoon water. Or, they may be coated with white icing. As a finishing touch, the pastries may be decorated with cherries or angelica or chopped nuts.

Danish envelopes

Roll the pastry ⅛ inch thick. Cut in 5 inch strips and cut the strips into squares. Place a spoonful of filling in the centre of each square, turn in the corners so that they meet in the centre and secure with a split almond or piece of angelica or candied peel. Brush with egg, and bake and finish as directed for crescents. Make sure to bake the 'envelopes' with the tip or apex underneath — this will keep them from unrolling while cooking.

Flaky pastry	**12 oz flour (350g)** ½ **teaspoon salt** **8 oz butter or margarine (225g)** ¼ **pint cold water (150ml)**

Sift the flour and salt. Cut in half the butter, add the water, mix lightly, and roll the dough into a rectangular shape, ¼ inch thick. Cut the rest of the butter into small pieces and spread over half of the dough, leaving a narrow margin. Fold over to cover the butter and press the edges together. Now fold the opposite sides to make 3 folds, one over and one underneath the butter layer. Roll out ¼ inch thick and fold as before. Reroll and fold again as directed. Roll ⅛ thick and use as required.

French flan pastry	**8 oz flour (225g)** ½ **teaspoon salt** ½**oz sugar (13g)** **6 oz butter or margarine (175g)** **1 egg yolk** **1 tablespoon lemon juice (15 ml)** **1 tablespoon water (15 ml)**

Sift the flour with the salt and sugar. Cut in the butter. Mix the egg yolk with the lemon juice and water, and add sufficient to the dry ingredients to form a stiff dough. Roll or pat the dough to ¼ inch thick.

French pastry (rich)

12 oz flour (350g)
4 oz butter or margarine (110g)
1 oz castor sugar (25g)
⅛ teaspoon salt
4 egg yolks

Place the flour in a heap on a pastry board and make a well in the centre. Cut the chilled butter into small dice and place, with the sugar, salt and egg yolks, in the centre of the flour. With the right hand, quickly work these ingredients, using the left hand to sprinkle in the flour as you work. Roll or pat the dough to ¼ inch thick.

Galette pastry

8 oz flour (225g)
½ teaspoon salt
½ oz castor sugar (13g)
6 oz butter or margarine (175g)
1 egg yolk
1 tablespoon water (15 ml)
1 dessertspoon lemon juice

Sift the flour with the salt and sugar, and rub in the butter. Add the egg yolk, beaten with the water and lemon juice. Chill thoroughly, then roll or pat until the dough is ½ inch thick. Place in a flan tin and chill again before filling and baking.

Puff pastry

1 lb flour (450g)
½ teaspoon salt
1 lb butter (450g)
½ pint iced water (275 ml)
1 teaspoon lemon juice

Puff pastry is expensive to make but a little goes a long way! It may be rolled out paper thin and will still puff up in the cooking.

Sift the flour with the salt. Cut ¼ of the butter into the flour, and mix with barely enough of the water and lemon juice to bind into small balls. Press these into one large ball and put aside to chill for 30 minutes. Cream the remainder of the butter until soft. Roll out on a floured board into a rectangular sheet. Divide the dough and roll into two sheets to fit the butter. Place the butter between the sheets of dough and press the edges together. Make three folds, one over and one underneath. Fold the other side in the same way, and chill for 1 hour. Roll thinly, but not so thinly that the butter breaks through. Fold and roll again, then fold and chill thoroughly. Fold and roll for three further times. When using, roll to ⅛ thick.

Raised pie pastry	8 oz flour (225g)
	½ teaspoon salt
	2 tablespoons water (30 ml)
	4 oz lard (110g)
	1 egg

Sift the flour with the salt. Boil the water, add the lard and stir until it is dissolved, then add to the flour and mix to a dough. The dough should be very dry; work it together until it adheres. Turn on to a floured board and knead like bread until the dough feels elastic. This kneading is necessary to make the pie keep its shape while cooking.

Line the bottom and sides of a deep round cake tin with ⅔ of the dough, moulding it well with the hands (keep the remainder warm in a cloth). Fill the pie with cubed pork, or veal or ham, or a mixture of all three, sprinkling seasonings between the layers. Do not add water. Pat out the remaining dough to make the lid, keeping back a small piece for decoration. Place the lid on the filled pie, pressing the edges together, and making a hole in the top to let the steam escape. Pat small pieces of dough flat and thin, cut into leaf shapes and mark 'veins' with knife. Place around the hole on the lid, being careful not to cover it. Brush with beaten egg. Bake for 1½–2 hours in a moderate oven (375°, gas mark 5) according to filling. When cold, pour liquid jelly into the pie through the hole in top, using a funnel.

Raised pies may also be baked without a tin. Mould ⅔ of the dough into a pie shape around a floured jar or large bottle. Fill and bake as above.

Shortcrust pastry (standard)	6 oz flour (185g)
	½ teaspoon salt
	1 teaspoon castor sugar
	4 oz butter or margarine (110g)
	2 tablespoons water (30 ml)

The quantities given are sufficient for an 8 inch or 9 inch one-crust pie. For a two-crust pie, double the amounts.

Sift the flour with the salt. Mix in the sugar, and cut in the butter. Sprinkle with the water and mix with a fork until all the flour is moistened. Gather the dough together and press it firmly into a ball. Roll to ¼ inch thick.

Shortcrust pastry (sweet for flans)	8 oz flour (225g)
	⅛ teaspoon salt
	4 oz butter or margarine (110g)
	3 oz castor sugar (75g)
	1 egg

Sift the flour with the salt. Rub in the butter and add the sugar. Add sufficient beaten egg to make a very stiff paste and roll out to ¼ inch thick. Do not grease the flan tin — good pastry makes this unnecessary. To lift the pastry, roll it around the rolling pin and unroll it on to the flan tin which has been turned upside down on a baking sheet. Press the dough to the sides of the pan and then trim it, leaving a rim of about 1 inch. Flute this rim with your fingers. Prick the dough with a fork and bake for 15 minutes at 425° (gas mark 7).

Note: If you cover the rolling pin with muslin, it will prevent the use of excess flour in rolling.

Strudel pastry (Austrian)	1 egg
	4 tablespoons warm water (60 ml)
	3 dessertspoons olive oil (20 ml)
	8 oz flour (225g)

Combine the egg, water and oil in a bowl. Beat well and add to the sieved flour. Knead thoroughly and roll until paper-thin.

Austrian apple strudel
Mix together 1 lb chopped apples (450g), 4 oz raisins (110g), 4 oz brown sugar (110g) and ½ teaspoon cinnamon, and spread on the pastry. Roll up carefully and cut into two pieces. Twist and bake in large tins in a 375° oven (gas mark 5) for 1 hour.

Strudel pastry (German)	12 oz flour (350g) ¼ teaspoon salt 1 egg 3 tablespoons warm water (45 ml) 2 tablespoons melted butter or margarine (30 ml)

Sift the flour and salt. Add the beaten egg and sufficient warm water to make a soft dough, combining the ingredients as quickly as possible. Knead on a floured board until the dough is elastic and no longer sticky. Then work in the melted butter. Cover with a warmed bowl and leave for 30 minutes. Cover a large table with a floured cloth. Gently pull and stretch the dough, placing both hands under it and pulling until it is paper-thin. The quantities given should make a square of dough measuring about 2 yards each way.

German apple strudel
Mix together with 2 lb finely chopped apple (900g), 4 oz each of currents and raisins (110g), 6 oz brown sugar (175g), 5 oz butter (160g), and 1½ teaspoons cinnamon, and spread on the pastry. Roll up as for a Swiss roll. To do this easily, fold one edge of the pastry over the filling; then lift the floured cloth and the pastry will roll itself up with just a little help. Cut into four sections. Twist each piece and place in large greased tins. Bake for 30 minutes at 400° (gas mark 6). Reduce the heat to 350° (gas mark 4) and bake for another 30 minutes or until the strudel is brown and crisp. Serve with cream.

Flans

For a professional finish to your flans, crimp the edges. Fill the flan dish (or sandwich tin) with the pastry, and trim evenly, allowing about 1 inch to overhang the edge. Fold this border up and back to make a standing rim and flute this between forefinger and thumb.

Flan cases can be baked either with the filling or 'blind', i.e. just the flan case. If any air is trapped there is a tendency for the base to rise. This can be avoided by pricking the base to allow any air to escape, by weighting it with beans or rice, or by putting a slightly smaller tin over the case.

Apricot glaze (for flans)

4 oz dried apricots (110g)
½ pint water (275 ml)
6 oz warmed sugar (175g)

To make a supply of glaze that will keep almost indefinitely, soak the apricots in the water for 12 hours. Bring slowly to the boil and add the warmed sugar. Stir until it is dissolved and simmer until the fruit is soft. Put through a sieve and store in a tightly sealed sterilized jar. When using the glaze, dilute to a spreading consistency with warm water.

Apple flan (French)

½ recipe French flan pastry
¼ pint milk (150g)
2 oz butter or margarine (50g)
5 oz castor sugar (150g)
1 oz sultanas (25g)
½ oz shredded almonds (13g)
½ oz chopped candied peel (13g)
1 teaspoon grated lemon rind
2 cups cooking apples
1 egg

Line a sandwich tin with the pastry. Heat the milk and melt the butter in it. Turn into a bowl and add 4 oz of the sugar, the sultanas, almonds, peel, lemon rind, and the apples which have been peeled and grated. Add the slightly beaten egg yolk, mix well, then fold in lightly the stiffly beaten egg white. Turn into the pastry-lined tin and bake for 30 minutes in a 475° oven (gas mark 9). When cooked, sprinkle the top thickly with the rest of the sugar.

Cherry flan

1 recipe sweet shortcrust pastry
1 lb cherries (450g)
4 oz castor sugar (110g)
1 tablespoon cornflour

Mix the sugar with the pitted cherries, and let them stand for about 1 hour or until the sugar has melted. Drain off the syrup — there should be about 6 tablespoons; if there is less, make up this amount with water. Blend 2 tablespoons of the syrup with the cornflour until smooth. Bring the rest of the syrup to a boil, stir in the cornflour and cook until the mixture is clear (about 2 minutes).

Roll the pastry to fit a 9 inch flan dish. Pat it into place and crimp the edges. Fill with the drained cherries and pour the syrup over. Bake for 40 minutes at 350° (gas mark 4).

Gooseberry flan

½ recipe galette pastry
1½ lb gooseberries (675g)
5 oz castor sugar (150g)

Roll or pat the dough to ⅛ thickness and place in a 9 inch flan dish and chill. Fill with the gooseberries (which you have topped and tailed) and the sugar. Bake for 25 minutes at 400° (gas mark 6). Cover with apricot glaze.

Plum custard flan

6 oz shortcrust pastry
12 oz plums (350g)
¼ teaspoon nutmeg
4 oz sugar (110g)
1 egg
3 oz flour (75g)
4 oz brown sugar (110g)
2 oz butter or margarine (50g)

Line a flan dish with the pastry and fill with the plums,

sprinkling them with the nutmeg and sugar. Beat the egg and pour it over the plums. Mix the flour, brown sugar and butter until crumbly, then sprinkle it over the fruit. Bake for 40 minutes at 425° (gas mark 7). Serve hot with cream.

Plum flan

1 recipe standard shortcrust pastry
12 oz plums (350g)
4 oz sugar (110g)
1 teaspoon cinnamon
1 oz butter or margarine (25g)

Spread the pastry in a 10 inch flan dish or baking tin. Fill with the plums, sprinkling them with the sugar and cinnamon. Dot with the butter and bake for 30 minutes at 425° (gas mark 7).

Strawberry flan

½ recipe sweet shortcrust pastry
2 tablespoons strawberry jam
8 oz strawberries (225g)
Whipped cream

Line a small flan dish or baking tin with the pastry and weight with beans or rice. Bake for 15 minutes at 425° (gas mark 7). When cold, spread the bottom of the flan with strawberry jam. Press halved strawberries into the jam and cover with whipped cream. Decorate with whole berries.

Strawberry flan (glazed)

½ recipe French flan pastry
2 lb strawberries (900g)
2 oz castor sugar (50g)
1 tablespoon lemon juice
1 tablespoon cornflour
Cochineal
Whipped cream

Line a flan dish or baking tin with the pastry, and bake for 15 minutes at 400° (gas mark 6). Cool and remove from tin.

Force half the hulled and crushed strawberries through a sieve and mix with the pulp, the sugar, lemon juice and the cornflour. Add a few drops of cochineal and cook in a double saucepan until thick and clear. Place the rest of the strawberries in the prepared flan case. Spread with the cooled strawberry mixture. Serve cold with whipped cream.

Patty shells

Patty shells make a quick and attractive dessert or tea-time pastry when filled with jam, chopped jelly, ice-cream, stewed or tinned fruit, confectioner's cream (add chopped nuts and/or raisins), cake crumbs mixed with jam or honey. Serve plain or topped with whipped cream.

Basic recipe	8 oz flour (225g)
	Pinch of salt
	4 oz butter or margarine (110g)
	2 oz castor sugar (50g)
	1 egg

Mix the flour and salt and sift into a basin. Rub in the butter until the mixture resembles breadcrumbs, and add the sugar. Stir in the beaten egg, adding a little cold water if necessary to make a stiff dough. Roll out ⅛ inch thick. Line patty tins, prick with a fork and bake in a very hot oven at 475° (gas mark 9) for about 8–10 minutes or until delicately browned.

Crimped patty shells are very decorative. Cut rounds of foil the same size as thinly-rolled rounds of pastry (about 3 inch across). Place the pastry on the foil. Put a small baking powder tin (or something similar) in the centre of the pastry and hold it there while you gather up the edges of the foil and pastry and flute them evenly. Bake as above.

Store cooked patty shells in an airtight container. Serve them cold or heated for 5 minutes in a 375° oven (gas mark 5).

Pies

Baked pie shell
Place a piece of greased paper in a pie plate lined with thinly rolled pastry. Weight with beans or rice. Bake for 15 minutes in a moderate oven at 350° (gas mark 4). Remove the paper and rice. When cold, fill as desired.

Double crust pie

Line a plate with shortcrust pastry, and fill with fruit, sugar, small dabs of butter and 1–2 tablespoons of flour (according to the juiciness of the fruit). If liked, a sprinkling of cinnamon may be added and/or a few cloves. Top with plain crust or lattice, brush with milk and bake in a hot oven (450°, gas mark 8) for 30–40 minutes. Dust with castor sugar.

Lattice topped pie

Roll half of the dough ⅛ inch thick. Fit it loosely in the pie plate, and trim it, leaving an inch overhanging the border. Fold this border up and back to make an upright rim, and flute it with your fingers. Roll the remaining dough ⅛ thick, cut it into narrow strips and arrange 7 or 8 strips over the top of the filled pie. Trim, moisten the ends and press into the fluted rim. Then arrange the same number of strips diagonally across the first strips, making diamond-shaped openings. Trim, moisten the ends and press into the rim. Brush with beaten egg yolk or milk and bake as usual.

Angel lemon pie

3 eggs
2 tablespoons lemon juice (30 ml)
⅛ tablespoon salt
6 oz sugar (150g)

Beat the yolks until thick, then add the lemon juice, the salt and half the sugar. Cook over boiling water until thick. Beat the egg whites until stiff and dry. Add the remaining sugar and fold into the cold custard. Pour into a baked pie shell and chill.

Apple pie (Dutch)

1 recipe standard shortcrust pastry
1 egg
1 lb cooking apples (450g)
Brown sugar
Cinnamon

Make standard shortcrust pastry, increasing the sugar to 1 tablespoon and using a beaten egg instead of the water. Roll the pastry about ¼ inch thick, form into an oblong and lay on a greased baking sheet. Press rows of apple slices into the pastry, sprinkle thickly with the brown sugar, dust with cinnamon and dot with butter. Bake for 30 minutes in a fairly hot oven at 425° (gas mark 7). Serve in slices or squares, with cream or custard.

Apple pie (glazed)	**1 recipe standard shortcrust pastry** **1 lb cooking apples (450g)** **4 oz sugar (110g)** **3 tablespoons water (45 ml)** **1 dessertspoon lemon juice** **½ teaspoon cinnamon** **1½ oz butter (40g)**

Make pastry for a 2 crust pie. Use half the pastry to line a 9 inch pie plate. Peel and slice the apples and mix them with the sugar and water. Cover and cook until they are tender but not mushy. Drain them, saving the juice and fill the pie dish. Sprinkle with lemon juice and cinnamon, and dot with butter. Make a lattice top, and bake for 30–35 minutes in a hot oven (425°, gas mark 7) or until the pastry is nicely browned. Cook the apple juice quickly in an uncovered saucepan until it is reduced by half. Pour this glaze over the top of the baked pie as soon as it comes from the oven.

Blackberry pie	**1 recipe standard shortcrust pastry** **1 lb blackberries (450g)** **3 oz sugar (75g)** **3 oz flour (75g)** **½ teaspoon cinnamon** **1 oz butter or margarine (25g)**

Pick over and hull the blackberries. Mix together the sugar, flour and cinnamon. Sprinkle this mixture over the black-berries and stir gently until they are well blended. Line an ungreased pie pan with half of the pastry, rolled ⅛ inch thick. Pour the fruit into the lined pie pan and dot with butter. Cover with pastry. Bake in a 450° oven (gas mark 8) for 10 minutes, then reduce the heat to 350° (gas mark 4), and continue baking until the pie is golden brown, about 40 minutes in all.

Fruit meringue pie

8 oz sugar (225g)
2 tablespoons water (30 ml)
½ teaspoon cream of tartar
⅛ teaspoon salt
2 egg whites
1 lb fruit (raspberries, loganberries, etc.) (450g)
2 oz castor sugar (50g)
1 baked pie shell

Put the sugar, water, cream of tartar, salt and the egg whites into a double boiler and beat steadily over rapidly boiling water until the meringue will hold a peak. Remove from the heat and continue to beat for about 3 minutes. Fill a baked pie shell with the fruit mixed with the sugar. Cover with the meringue, swirling it around the top with a spoon for a professional finish. Place under the grill for 2 minutes to colour the top slightly. Serve cold.

Gooseberry pie

10 oz flour (275g)
¾ teaspoon salt
6 oz butter or margarine (175g)
2 tablespoons water (30 ml)
1½ oz soft butter or margarine (40g)
1 lb gooseberries (450g)
6 oz sugar (150g)
½ teaspoon cinnamon

Sift the flour with the salt. Cut the butter into the flour until the particles are the size of large peas. Sprinkle with water, a dessertspoon at a time, and mix lightly with a fork until all the flour is moistened. Gather the dough together with your fingers so that it leaves the sides of the bowl clean, and press firmly into a ball. Divide into two parts, one slightly larger than the other. Line a pie dish with the smaller portion and brush with melted butter. Fill with topped and tailed gooseberries, mixed with the sugar and cinnamon. Cover with the rest of the pastry. Bake for 40–45 minutes at 425° (gas mark 7).

Gooseberry pie (spiced)

1 recipe standard shortcrust pastry
1 lb gooseberries (450g)
6 oz sugar (175g)
4 tablespoons water (60 ml)
1 oz flour (25g)
$\frac{1}{8}$ teaspoon salt
$\frac{1}{2}$ teaspoon cinnamon
$\frac{1}{2}$ teaspoon ground cloves
$\frac{1}{2}$ teaspoon nutmeg
1 tablespoon butter

Cook the gooseberries in 4 oz of sugar and water until tender. Combine the remaining 2 oz of sugar with the flour, salt spices. Stir into the cooked fruit and cool. Line a pie plate with half of the pastry. Fill with the fruit mixture, dot with butter, and finish with a lattice top. Bake in a hot oven for 40 minutes (425°, gas mark 7).

Mince pies

8 oz puff pastry (225g)
12 oz mincemeat (350g)
1 egg
1 tablespoon milk (15g)

Roll the pastry very thinly and cut into 3 inch rounds with a floured cutter. Place a dessertspoon of mincemeat in the centre of half of the rounds. Wet the edges. Cover with the other halves and press the edges together with a fork. Brush with the beaten egg and milk, taking care that the egg does not go over the sides of the pies as this would seal the pastry and prevent it from puffing. Placed on a rinsed and well-drained baking sheet and bake in a hot oven at 475° (gas mark 9) for 8–10 minutes, or until the pastry has reached its full height; then reduce heat to 350° (gas mark 4) and bake for another 10–15 minutes longer until browned.

Mince pies can be reheated in a moderate oven (350°, gas mark 4). Time: 7–10 minutes.

Plum pie

½ recipe flaky pastry
1¼ lb plums (560g)
4 oz sugar (110g)
4 tablespoons water (60 ml)
A little milk
1 oz castor sugar (25g)

Roll out the pastry large enough to make a lid for a pie dish. Put the plums into the dish, sprinkling each layer with sugar, finishing with a layer of plums. Add the water. Moisten the rim of the pie dish and lay the pastry lid over the plums, taking care not to stretch it (otherwise it will shrink from the rim during the cooking). Press the pastry on to the rim, trim carefully from underneath with a sharp knife and mark all around with the prongs of a fork. Brush the top of the pie with milk, make a slight slit to allow the steam to escape, and bake for 40 minutes at 375° (gas mark 5). Then turn oven down to 325° (gas mark 3) and bake for another 20 minutes. Sprinkle while hot with castor sugar.

Raspberry pie

1 recipe standard shortcrust pastry
1¼ lb raspberries (560g)
¼ teaspoon salt
4 oz sugar (110g)
1 tablespoon flour
1 tablespoon butter or margarine
1 tablespoon milk (15 ml)
1 dessertspoon lemon juice.

Combine the fruit and the dry ingredients. Line a pie plate with half of the pastry, fill with the fruit mixture, dot with butter and sprinkle with lemon juice. Cover with the remainder of the pastry, brush with milk, and bake for 40 minutes at 425° (gas mark 7).

Rhubarb lemon pie

1 recipe standard shortcrust pastry
1½ lb diced rhubarb (675g)
6 oz sugar (175g)
1 tablespoon flour

1 egg
¾ teaspoon grated lemon rind
1 tablespoon lemon juice (15 ml)
4 tablespoons water (60 ml)

Line a pie plate with half of the pastry and fill with the diced rhubarb. Combine the sugar and the flour, stir in the beaten egg, lemon rind, lemon juice and water, and cook over boiling water until slightly thickened. Pour over the rhubarb and top with a lattice crust. Bake for 45 minutes at 425° (gas mark 7).

Shoo-fly pie   **½ recipe standard shortcrust pastry**
4 oz butter or margarine (110g)
4 oz sugar (110g)
2 egg yolks
1 cup stale breadcrumbs
¼ pint milk (150 ml)
8 oz stewed or tinned fruit (225g)

Roll out the pastry ⅛ inch thick, and line a pie plate. Bake 'blind' in the oven for about 15 minutes at 450° (gas mark 8). Cream the butter and sugar. Add the egg yolks, and mix in the egg crumbs which have been soaked in enough milk to moisten. Add the fruit and mix well. Turn into the baked pie shell and bake in a slow oven at 300° (gas mark 2) until firm.

Tarts and tartlets

Apple tartlets   **8 oz shortcrust pastry (225g)**
(jellied)   **2 oz sugar (50g)**
½ pint water (275 ml)
6 whole cloves
2 cups sliced apples
Cochineal
1 dessertspoon powdered gelatine
Whipped cream

Roll out the pastry about ⅛ inch thick. Line 12 greased patty tins with the pastry. Prick well with a fork and bake for 10 minutes in a 425° oven (gas mark 7). Boil the sugar with the water and the cloves for 5 minutes. Take out the cloves. Simmer the apples in the syrup until tender but not broken, then lift out the fruit with a fish slice and colour the syrup pale pink with a few drops of cochineal. Now add the gelatine (or a half packet of lemon-flavoured jelly). Stir until dissolved and leave until cold. Fill the cooked pastry cases with the apple, cover with the syrup and leave until set. Decorate with whipped cream.

Any fruit can be substituted for apples.

Apple ginger tarts

12 oz shortcrust pastry (350g)
½ cup whipped cream
1 cup thick apple puree
1 oz preserved ginger (25g)

Make 18 small tartlet cases with the pastry and bake. Combine the cream with the sweetened apple puree and the chopped ginger, and fill the tartlets.

This mixture is delicious as a topping for squares of butter sponge mixture or for a butter sponge sandwich.

Banbury cakes

8 oz puff or flaky pastry (225g)
6 oz mincemeat (175g)
1 tablespoon beaten egg
2 tablespoons castor sugar

Roll out the pastry very thinly and cut in rounds, using a small tea-plate as a guide. Put a generous spoonful of mincemeat in the centre of each round. Brush around the edges with cold water, fold in on four sides to close and pinch edges firmly together. Turn so that the raw edges are underneath and press to flatten to a round. Place on a baking tin and bake for 12 minutes in a very hot oven at 475° (gas mark 9). Sprinkle with castor sugar while hot.

Cheesecakes (mincemeat)

4 oz butter or margarine (110g)
4 oz castor sugar (110g)
½ teaspoon grated lemon rind
1 dessertspoon lemon juice
1 tablespoon ground almonds

2 eggs
4 oz flour (110g)
1 teaspoon baking powser
8 oz puff or shortcrust pastry (225g)
4 oz mincemeat (110g)

Beat the butter until creamy, gradually adding the sugar and beat until fluffy. Beat in the lemon rind and juice, the ground almonds and the eggs. Add the flour sifted with the baking powder. Line patty tins with the pastry. Put a spoonful of mincemeat in each and three-quarters fill with the creamed mixture. Bake for 15–20 minutes at 450° (gas mark 38).

Cheesecakes (spiced)

¼ pint milk (150 ml)
3 oz breadcrumbs
2 eggs
1 oz butter or margarine (25g)
3 oz castor sugar (75g)
⅛ teaspoon nutmeg
⅛ teaspoon cinnamon
2 tablespoons currants
4 oz shortcrust pastry (110g)

Pour the boiling milk over the breadcrumbs and leave to soak for 15 minutes. Separate the eggs. Cream the butter and beat in the cooled breadcrumbs. Add the sugar, spices and currants, and mix well. Then beat in the egg yolks and lastly the stiffly beaten whites. Line some patty tins with pastry, half fill with the cheesecake mixture and bake for 15 minutes at 450° (gas mark 8).

Gooseberry tartlets

Invented by Emily, first Duchess of Leinster, for her favourite son, Lord Edward Fitzgerald.

12 oz flour (350g)
$\frac{1}{4}$ teaspoon salt
4 oz butter or margarine (110g)
4 oz sugar (110g)
1 egg
1 teaspoon vanilla
1 tablespoon cream or top of milk

2 egg yolks
1 cup stewed gooseberries
1 oz melted butter (25g)

Sift the dry ingredients. Cream the butter and sugar, and add the egg, vanilla and cream. Gradually add in the flour mixture. Chill the dough thoroughly in the fridge or a very cool place. Place on a lightly floured board and roll out $\frac{1}{8}$ inch thick. Line patty tins with the dough and fill with gooseberry curd. Cover with lids of pastry and bake for 15 minutes at 375° (gas mark 5).

To make the curd, mix the egg yolks with 1 cup of stewed gooseberries, sweetened and sieved, and add the melted butter. Cook over boiling water until thick.

Jam puffs

Cut thin puff pastry into large rounds. Place a little raspberry jam in the centre. Fold over from three sides to the centre. Brush with egg white, sprinkle with sugar and bake for 12 minutes at 450° (gas mark 8).

Maids of honour

8 oz puff pastry (225g)
4 oz butter or margarine (110g)
$1\frac{1}{2}$ tablespoons lemon juice (20 ml)
2 teaspoons grated lemon rind
4 oz castor sugar (110g)
1 tablespoon fine breadcrumbs
1 egg

Roll out the pastry very thin and line small patty tins. Work the dough towards the top of the tins so that it is thickish around the rims and paper-thin at the sides and bottom.

Melt the butter over a low heat, add the lemon juice, rind, sugar and breadcrumbs. Add the well-beaten egg and cook over hot water, stirring occasionally until the mixture thickens (on no account must it be allowed to boil). When the filling is cold, fill the lined patty tins not more than two-thirds full (the pastry should close in over the filling in the cooking. Bake for 15 minutes at 450° (gas mark 8).

Mince tart

8 oz shortcrust pastry (225g)
8 oz mincemeat (225g)
1½ cups sweetened stewed apple
½ cup drained and crushed pineapple
1 egg (beaten)
Castor sugar

Divide the pastry into two and roll ⅛ inch thick. With one half, line a pie dish. Combine the mincemeat with the apple and pineapple and fill the pie with this mixture. Cover with a lattice top. Brush with beaten egg and bake for 35 minutes at 450° (gas mark 6). Sprinkle with castor sugar and serve hot.

Mincemeat tartlets

8 oz shortcrust pastry (225g)
¼ pint milk (275 ml)
3 oz breadcrumbs
1 oz butter or margarine (25g)
3 oz mincemeat (75g)
1 oz sugar (25g)
2 eggs

Bring the milk to the boil and pour over the breadcrumbs. Add the melted butter, mincemeat and sugar, and mix well. Separate the eggs. Beat the yolks well and the whites until stiff and dry. When the breadcrumb mixture is cold beat in the yolks and then fold in the whites. Line small tart tins with the thinly rolled pastry, three-quarters fill with the mincemeat mixture and bake for 15 minutes at 450° (gas mark 8).

Index